BOATsmart!®

Boating Safety Info Line: 1-877-792-3926
info@BoatSmartExam.com
www.BoatSmartExam.com®

Printed in Canada
Written by OUTDOORsmart!™
ISBN 0-9734023-0-X

BOATsmart!® is a proud member of the Canadian Safe Boating Council

DISCLAIMER

The navigation and right-of-way rules contained in this course summarize basic navigation rules for which a boat operator is responsible. Additional and more in-depth rules apply regarding various types of waterways and operation in relation to commercial vessels and other watercraft. It is the responsibility of a boat operator to know and follow all navigation rules as required by the Collision Regulations.

CONGRATULATIONS!

Thank you for making the choice to boat smart! By learning the information in this Study Guide, you'll obtain the knowledge you need to obtain your Pleasure Craft Operator Card and boat with confidence.

IN THIS STUDY GUIDE YOU'LL LEARN EVERYTHING YOU NEED TO:

> Understand boating basics and terminology

> Understand the acts, codes and regulations that govern Canada's waterways

> Equip your boat with the right equipment and know how to use it

> Properly maintain your vessel and its equipment

> Share the waterways and operate your watercraft in a safe and responsible manner

> Have confidence when navigating amongst other boat traffic during the day or at night

> Be able to recognize the different markers and buoys and navigate using Canada's Aids to Navigation System

> Know how to respond in emergency situations

GET CERTIFIED
PLEASURE CRAFT OPERATOR CARD

A Pleasure Craft Operator Card (PCOC) proves that you have obtained the knowledge to safely operate a motorized pleasure craft on Canada's waterways.

Commonly referred to as a 'boating license', the official PCOC is issued upon successful completion of a Transport Canada Boating Safety Test.

WHEN DO YOU NEED A PCOC?
IMMEDIATELY!

If you operate any motorized watercraft you require a PCOC*. This federal requirement applies to all operators of motorized watercraft regardless of age, length of boat or engine horsepower – including electric trolling motors and sailboats equipped with engines. There is no minimum age to obtain an Operator Card and once certified your PCOC is good for life.

ALL BOATS WITH ENGINES   ALL AGES

Boaters who fail to carry a PCOC* can be fined a minimum of $250 by any officer of the peace.

*Pleasure Craft Operator Card or proof of competency. See page 22 for details.

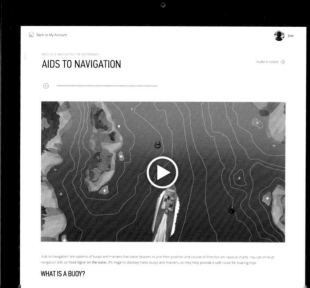

ONLINE COURSE & OFFICIAL TEST

BoatSmartExam.com®

The BOATsmart!® Online Course is fully narrated and includes animated and interactive lessons.

  Watch, listen and learn, from anywhere on any device.

 We'll automatically track your progress.

 Available 24/7 and perfect for all ages.

 Go boating today! Print a Temp Card immediately when you pass.

 Standard one-time fee includes free retries and mailing of your official PCOC.

BOATsmart!
AT CANADIAN TIRE

TESTING LOCATIONS

For a complete list of BOATsmart!® Testing Centres and Safe Boating Team Events visit BoatSmartExam.com®.

As a Transport Canada Accredited Course Provider, BOATsmart® has partnered with Canadian Tire to offer the Boating Safety Test in local communities.

Look for BOATsmart!® Safe Boating Teams at:
> Participating Canadian Tire Locations
> Boat Shows and Community Events
> BOATsmart!® Certified Testing Centres

IT'S YOUR TIME
BOATsmart!

We're boaters too, so we get it. It's about your time. Out on the water with family and friends. Sharing experiences and making the most of your time together. That's why we created the concept of Boater Enjoyment – it's central to everything we do.

OUR MISSION

BOATsmart!®'s mission is to empower you to boat with confidence.

EDUCATION & REFRESHER LESSONS

BOATsmart!® administers the Transport Canada Boating Safety Course and Test in-class, on-water, and online for the Pleasure Craft Operator Card.

BoatSmartExam.com®

Boater Enjoyment

RECREATIONAL BOAT INSURANCE

BOATsmart! Assure™ is best-in-class insurance for recreational boats and watercraft. BOATsmart!® cardholders save up to 25% off their annual policy premium.

BoatSmartAssure.com™

BOATING SAFETY EQUIPMENT

BOATsmart! Marine Safety™ Products are designed and manufactured with innovation, dependability and quality. From our Boating Safety Bailer Kit that doesn't leak, to our exclusive new Wallet Buoy license holder, our products work when you need them most.

BoatSmartMarine.com™

WATCH LESSONS COME ALIVE

We've included layers of enhanced digital, animated and interactive content. All right on top of the printed page.

HERE'S HOW IT WORKS:

STEP 1: Download the free Layar App

STEP 2: Look for the Layar symbol on select pages

STEP 3: Scan the page with the Layar App

STEP 4: Exclusive digital content including animation, narration and enhanced video will display on your device layered overtop of the printed page

**UNLOCK
INTERACTIVE
CONTENT**

When you see this tab, scan the page with the Layar App

BOAT WITH CONFIDENCE

BOATsmart! Marine Safety™ Products help you boat with confidence knowing that you've got quality, innovation and dependability on your side. You can count on BOATsmart! Marine Safety™ Products to work when you need them most.

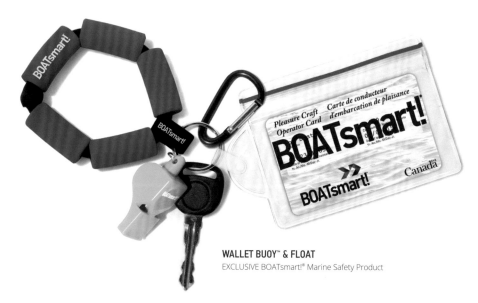

WALLET BUOY™ & FLOAT
EXCLUSIVE BOATsmart!® Marine Safety Product

BOATsmart!
MARINE SAFETY

Quality · Innovation · Dependability

BOATsmart! | assure

COMPARE & SAVE

GET A NO OBLIGATION ONLINE QUOTE AND SEE EXACTLY HOW MUCH YOU'LL SAVE ON BOAT INSURANCE. TRY IT

American

TSA PRECHK

oneworld

BOARDING PASS

DOORS CLOSE 10 MINUTES PRIOR TO DEPARTURE

PASSENGER NAME
ROGAN/EVELYN

FREQUENT FLYER #

RECORD LOCATOR
XKQDZS

FROM:
TORONTO

TO:
CHICAGO OHARE

FLIGHT	CLASS	DATE	DEPARTS
AA3516	N	13MAR	310P

	GATE	BOARDING TIME	SEAT
GROUP 5	A9	225P	3C

MAIN

0012118675798

CA033

American

BOARDING PASS
ROGAN/EVELYN

FROM:
TORONTO

TO:
CHICAGO OHARE

FLIGHT	SEAT
AA3516	3C

GROUP 5

DATE	CLASS	DEPARTS
13MAR	N	310P

American oneworld BOARDING PASS American

DOORS CLOSE 10 MINUTES PRIOR TO DEPARTURE

PASSENGER NAME
ROGAN/DAVID

FREQUENT FLYER #

RECORD LOCATOR
XKQDZS

BOARDING PASS
ROGAN/DAVID

FROM:
TORONTO

TO:
CHICAGO OHARE

FLIGHT	CLASS	DATE	DEPARTS
AA3516	N	13MAR	310P

FROM:
TORONTO

TO:
CHICAGO OHARE

GROUP 5

	GATE	BOARDING TIME	SEAT
	A9	225P	3B

MAIN

0012118675790

CA014

FLIGHT SEAT
AA3516 3B

GROUP 5

DATE	CLASS	DEPARTS
13MAR	N	310P

INSURANCE FOR SMART BOATERS

BEST-IN-CLASS COVERAGE FOR LESS

We're changing boat insurance. For the better.

There's a new way to buy boat insurance. Best-in-class coverage at a better price. Fast and transparent claims settlements. Great customer service. Compare and save when you buy direct from BOATsmart! Assure™. Smart boaters like you are making the switch everyday.

GET A FREE ONLINE QUOTE TODAY >

BoatSmartAssure.com™
1-855-829-6753

Underwritten by Lloyd's of London, distributed (brokered) by McLean and Dickey Ltd.

BOATsmart!®'s
5 PRINCIPLES OF BOATING SAFETY:

GET THE KNOWLEDGE
Take personal responsibility, learn the skills and acquire the knowledge you need to boat with confidence. Ensure that you understand the "rules of the road" and how to boat safely.

WEAR A LIFE JACKET
Always wear your life jacket or PFD and make sure your passengers do the same.

DON'T DRINK AND BOAT
Use common sense, take responsibility for your actions and set a good example for others. Always say NO to drinking and boating and operate your boat responsibly at all times.

BE PREPARED
Equip yourself, your boat and your passengers with the right safety gear and know how to use it. Check the weather and boating environment before heading out.

BE CONFIDENT
Be prepared for an emergency and know how to react in unexpected situations.

When you are ready to take your official Transport Canada Boating Safety Test, visit **BoatSmart**Exam.com.

ACKNOWLEDGEMENTS

BOATsmart!® was fortunate to have the support and assistance of many partner organizations and individuals who contributed to the development of this study guide. Our sincere appreciation and thanks for their generous investment of time, creativity and insight.

ATLANTIC MARINE TRADES ASSOCIATION

BOATING ONTARIO

BRITISH COLUMBIA MARINE TRADES ASSOCIATION

CANADIAN SAFE BOATING COUNCIL

MID-CANADA MARINE DEALERS ASSOCIATION

NATIONAL MARINE MANUFACTURES ASSOCIATION

CANADIAN COAST GUARD

ONTARIO PROVINCIAL POLICE

ROYAL CANADIAN MOUNTED POLICE

SÛRETÉ DU QUÉBEC

TRANSPORT CANADA

Contents

MODULE 01

BOATING IN CANADA: BOATING BASICS

MODULE 02

BOATING RULES, REGULATIONS AND EQUIPMENT

MODULE 03

BEFORE HEADING OUT

MODULE 04

SAFE BOAT OPERATION

Contents

MODULE 05

NAVIGATION & RIGHT-OF-WAY RULES

MODULE 06

MARKERS AND BUOYS

MODULE 07

EMERGENCY PREPAREDNESS

RESOURCES

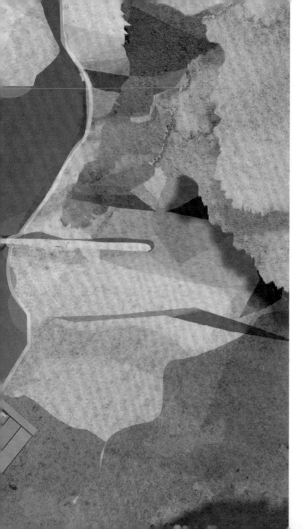

module 1
BOATING IN CANADA: BOATING BASICS

> Rules and Regulations
> Operator Competency
> Competency Requirements
> Age and Horsepower Restrictions
> The Basics
> Boating Terminology
> Module 1 Summary and Quiz

BOATING IN CANADA

Canadians love hitting the waterways and recreational boating has become a favourite pastime for many. In fact, there are over 9 million recreational boaters in Canada. Sadly, not all boaters survive. On average there are 120 boating fatalities in Canada per year and there are thousands of unreported non-fatal accidents occurring each year. What's worse is that most of these deaths were preventable as they were caused by a lack of basic boating knowledge and skill.

By choosing to complete this Study Guide and obtain your Pleasure Craft Operator Card (PCOC), you've made the choice to enhance boating safety and fun for all!

IT'S EVERYONE'S RESPONSIBILITY

All boaters in Canada are responsible for knowing and obeying the rules and regulations that apply on Canadian waterways. Boat operators should understand the most common causes of boating accidents and fatalities in Canada:

1. **Not wearing a life jacket or personal flotation device (PFD)**
2. Person overboard (falling overboard)
3. Capsizing (sinking, swamping, grounding) and collisions with other boats
4. Operating a vessel while impaired by drugs or alcohol

OPERATOR TRAINING AND CERTIFICATION

On **April 1, 1999,** the Canadian Coast Guard enacted the Competency of Operators Pleasure Craft Regulations. These regulations require that boat operators obtain proof of competency, such as a **Pleasure Craft Operator Card (PCOC).**

IT'S THE LAW

As of September 15, 2009, **operators of motorized vessels including personal watercraft (PWCs), motorized sailboats and small boats with electric trolling motors are required to carry proof of competency. The proof of competency must be carried onboard at all times.** A photocopy of your Pleasure Craft Operator Card is not acceptable. **There are no exemptions for engine size, length of boat or age of boat operator.**

For more information on the *Competency of Operators of Pleasure Craft Regulations*, please contact BOATsmart!®

BoatSmartExam.com®

1-877-792-3926

PROOF OF COMPETENCY

You may be asked to provide proof of competency to local law enforcement agencies when operating on your local waterway. Proof of competency can take 3 forms:

1. A **Pleasure Craft Operator Card** issued following the successful completion of a Transport Canada Accredited exam
2. Proof of having taken a boating safety course in Canada prior to April 1, 1999, or having obtained an approved marine certificate*
3. A completed rental boat safety checklist (required for operating any rental boat that is motorized)

*Visit www.boatingsafety.gc.ca or call 1-800-267-6687 to learn more.

COMPETENCY REQUIREMENTS

Operators of motorized vessels in Canada are required to carry proof of competency on board at all times – regardless of age, size of boat or engine horsepower. Operators should also always carry personal identification.

NON-RESIDENTS

Non-residents who operate non-Canadian registered vessels for less than 45 consecutive days do not require proof of competency. However, non-residents who operate a Canadian registered vessel must carry proof of competency at all times. Proof of residency is required.

WHAT IF I DON'T HAVE PROOF OF COMPETENCY?

If you cannot provide proof of competency to a law enforcement officer, you will face a minimum $250.00 fine plus administrative fees.

OBTAINING A PLEASURE CRAFT OPERATOR CARD (PCOC)

BOATsmart!® administers the official Transport Canada Boating Safety Test. Boaters who score a passing grade of 75% or higher on the test will receive their Pleasure Craft Operator Card. Once obtained, your BOATsmart!® PCOC is good for life.

ONLINE COURSE & TEST

The BOATsmart!® Online Course is the most convenient way to prepare for the test and obtain your PCOC. You can complete the narrated, animated study guide from the comfort of home at your own pace.

STEP 1 Visit BoatSmartExam.com®

STEP 2 Complete the BOATsmart!® Online Course. Study at your own pace and the BOATsmart!® system will track your progress.

STEP 3 Take the official Boating Safety Test online from the comfort of home. No supervisor is required.

STEP 4 Print a temporary card immediately and receive your permanent PCOC by mail.

BOATsmart!® also offers in-class and on-water courses in local communities. Visit **BoatSmart**Exam.com® for details and locations.

AGE AND HORSEPOWER RESTRICTIONS

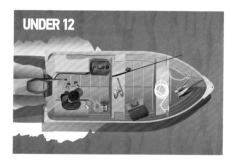

UNDER 12 YEARS OF AGE

Boaters under 12 years of age, with proof of competency, can operate a boat without supervision so long as the engine is not more than 10 hp. **Operators under 12 years of age are NOT allowed to operate a Personal Watercraft (PWC) under any conditions.**

12 TO UNDER 16 YEARS OF AGE

Boaters 12 to under 16 years of age, with proof of competency, can operate a boat without supervision as long as the engine is not more than 40 hp. **Operators 12 to under 16 years of age are NOT allowed to operate a PWC under any conditions.**

16 YEARS OF AGE AND OLDER

Operators 16 years of age or older can operate a boat without supervision or horsepower restrictions. They can also operate a PWC provided they have obtained proof of competency.

SUPERVISION PROVISIONS

All younger boat operators who require direct supervision, under the Age and Horsepower Restrictions, must carry proof of competency on board the boat. Their supervisor must be on the boat and must be at least 16 years of age or older. Operators under 16 years of age are not permitted to operate a PWC, even if supervised.

WHO IS THE 'OPERATOR'?

A boat 'operator' is considered to be the person who is in control of the pleasure craft and who is responsible for it's operation. As a pleasure craft operator you are responsible for yourself, your passengers, your vessel and the safety of your fellow boaters.

WHAT IS A 'PLEASURE CRAFT'?

A 'pleasure craft' is any boat that is used exclusively for pleasure or recreation.
If the boat carries goods or passengers for profit, payment, reward or hire, it is considered to be a 'commercial craft' and is subject to different rules and regulations.

WHAT IS A 'POWER-DRIVEN CRAFT'?

Any boat powered by a motor or engine is a 'power-driven craft'. This includes motorized sailboats.

WHAT IS A 'NON-POWERED CRAFT'?

A non-powered boat operates **without a motor or engine** (such as a canoe, a rowboat or a sailboat under the power of sail).

WHAT IS A 'PERSONAL WATERCRAFT'?

A personal watercraft (PWC) is equipped with an inboard engine and is powered by a jet-propulsion system. PWCs have unique handling characteristics because of their size and method of power. For example, **you cannot steer a PWC unless throttle power is applied.**

WHAT IS A 'SAILING VESSEL'?

A sailing vessel or sailboat is **any boat that is under the power of sail**. If a sailboat is powered with an engine, it is considered to be a motorized boat and is subject to the same rules and regulations that apply to 'power-driven' vessels.

SAFE BOATING TIP

Boaters are required to know the difference between 'power-driven' craft, 'sail-powered' craft and 'non-powered' craft. Different navigation and equipment rules apply for each type of craft.

THE HULL

The 'hull' is the portion of the boat that rides both in and on top of the water. **The hull does not include any masts, sails, rigging, machinery or equipment.**

THERE ARE 3 GENERAL HULL TYPES:

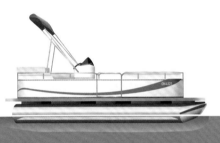

PLANING HULL:

Designed to **glide on the surface of the water** as the boat gains speed (like most powerboats).

PONTOON HULL:

Utilizes two or more **pontoons to create lift and flotation**.

DISPLACEMENT HULL:

Designed to power through the water and often found on larger boats (like sailboats).

HULL STYLES

The shape of a boat's hull greatly affects the way it moves through the water.
Operators should be able to identify different hull styles and recognize the unique handling characteristics of each:

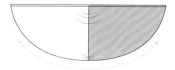 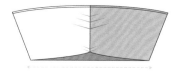 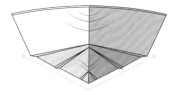 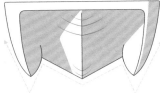

ROUND-BOTTOM:

Typical to sailboats and canoes, round-bottom hulls are not as stable and tend to 'roll' in waves. You should be cautious when loading, entering and exiting a round-bottom boat as it may roll easily.

FLAT-BOTTOM:

Like a barge, these boats are generally designed for slow speeds and calm water. Flat bottom boats tend to be less stable than other hull types in rough water.

DEEP 'V' BOTTOM:

The most common type of power-boat hull, these boats move through rough water at higher speeds and have a smoother ride than other hull types.

MULTI-CHINE HULL:

Multi-chine hull boats, such as catamarans, are very stable but can be more difficult to manoeuver.

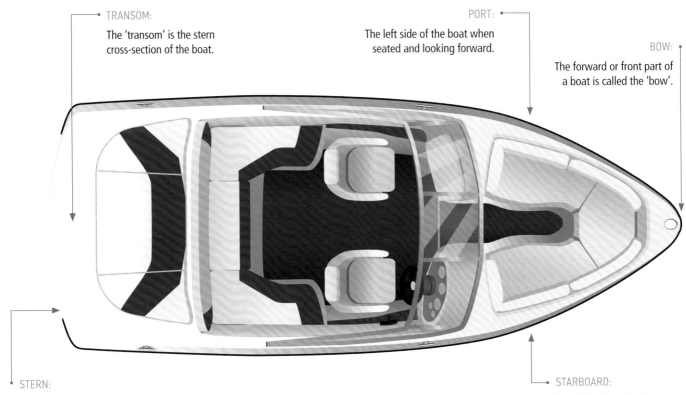

TRANSOM:
The 'transom' is the stern cross-section of the boat.

PORT:
The left side of the boat when seated and looking forward.

BOW:
The forward or front part of a boat is called the 'bow'.

STERN:
The rear section of a boat is called the 'stern'.

STARBOARD:
The right side of the boat when seated and looking forward.

Memory Tip: Can't remember which side of your boat is 'port' or 'starboard'? You'll like this rule of thumb: The word 'port' has 4 letters. So does the word 'left'. This trick should help you to remember that port is the left side of the boat when looking forward! (LEFT/PORT)

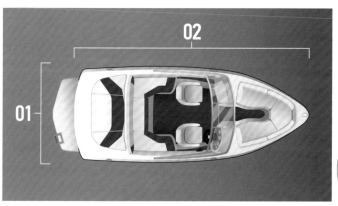

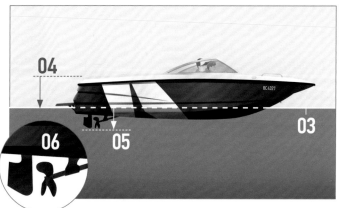

01 BEAM:

The beam is the width of a boat at its widest point.

02 LENGTH:

A boat's length is the distance from the tip of the bow to the farthest point on the stern (front to back, measured in a straight line). The length excludes the swim platform.

03 WATERLINE:

On the boat's hull, this is the line at which the boat sits in the water when the boat is properly loaded with passengers and equipment.

04 FREEBOARD:

'Freeboard' is the height of a boat's side, from the waterline to the deck.

05 DRAFT:

'Draft' is the depth of water that a boat needs in order to float freely. A boat's draft is measured as the distance from the waterline to the lowest point of the boat.

06 PROPELLER:

This piece of equipment, also known as the 'prop', rotates and powers a boat forward or backward.

SAFETY LANYARD & ON/OFF SWITCH:

The safety lanyard is attached to the on/off switch at one end and to the operator at the other end. If you fall off the PWC, the lanyard will release and the engine will shut down immediately.

HANDLEBARS AND THROTTLE:

Steer the PWC by turning the handlebars and applying throttle.

SEAT:

The driver and passengers should be seated at all times.

ON 4321

JET THRUST NOZZLE:

High-powered water propels the PWC through the jet thrust nozzle. Never start the engine or operate the PWC if a passenger is positioned behind the nozzle.

JET INTAKE:

Water enters the jet intake where it passes through a high-speed impeller to propel the PWC. Use caution when near the intake—loose items such as clothing and long hair can be ingested through the intake by the force of the water and rotating impeller.

ENGINE TYPES

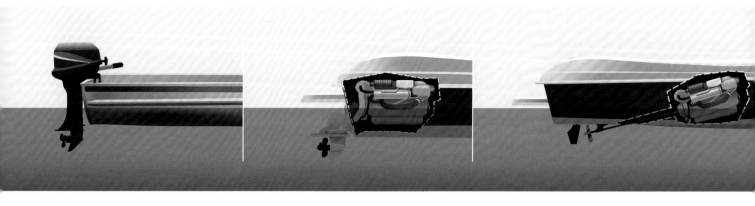

OUTBOARD ENGINE

An 'outboard engine' is attached to the transom (stern) of a boat. The operator steers the boat by moving the entire engine and drive assembly. In order to avoid hitting bottom in shallow areas, the engine can be moved up or down, manually or electronically.

INBOARD/OUTBOARD ENGINE

An 'inboard/outboard engine' is mounted within the hull of the boat and the lower unit of the engine (or the propeller and drive assembly) is mounted on the transom (outside) of the boat. The operator steers the boat by moving the wheel from left to right.

INBOARD ENGINE

With 'inboard engines', the motor and most of the drive assembly are mounted within the hull of the boat. This means that only the propeller and propeller shaft are outside of the hull. When the operator moves the steering wheel, a rudder attached at the stern (not the engine itself) changes the direction of the boat's movement.

MODULE 1 SUMMARY

By obtaining your Pleasure Craft Operator Card you can legally operate a motorized vessel in Canada with the knowledge and skills you need to boat safely and be confident while on the water. You must also have knowledge of basic boating terminology, engine types and the diverse types of pleasure craft you may operate or encounter while boating. You should understand the limitations and handling characteristics of the different types of pleasure craft that operate in Canada's waterways.

MODULE 1 QUIZ

1   WHICH OF THE FOLLOWING FACTORS IS THE NUMBER ONE CAUSE OF BOATING-RELATED FATALITIES IN CANADA?

A   Collision with another boat
B   Capsizing emergencies
C   Not wearing a life jacket or PFD
D   Alcohol consumption

2   WHICH TYPE OF VESSEL REQUIRES YOU TO CARRY PROOF OF COMPETENCY, SUCH AS A PLEASURE CRAFT OPERATOR CARD, ON BOARD AT ALL TIMES, WHEN OPERATING?

A   All pleasure craft fitted with a motor
B   Paddle craft that are powered by a sail or by oars
C   Wind-powered sailboats that are greater than 9 feet in length
D   All vessels that weigh over 10 tons and are greater than 9 feet in length

3   WHICH OF THE FOLLOWING IS THE CORRECT DEFINITION OF A 'PLEASURE CRAFT'?

A   Any vessel, ship, boat or other type of craft that is used exclusively for pleasure or recreation
B   Any vessel, ship, boat or other type of craft
C   Any vessel, ship, boat or other type of craft that is used for commercial reasons
D   Any vessel, ship, boat or other type of craft that can carry passengers

MODULE 1 QUIZ

4   WHICH OF THE FOLLOWING IS THE CORRECT DEFINITION FOR THE 'PORT' SIDE OF A BOAT?

A   To the left side of your vessel when looking forward
B   To the right side of your vessel when looking forward
C   The front of the vessel
D   The rear of the vessel

5   WHAT IS THE MINIMUM AGE TO OPERATE A PERSONAL WATERCRAFT (PWC)?

A   18
B   21
C   16
D   15

6   WHAT IS THE FRONT OF A BOAT CALLED?

A   Beam
B   Bow
C   Gunwale
D   Bilge

7   WHAT IS THE BACK OF A BOAT CALLED?

A   Astern
B   Freeboard
C   Bow
D   Stern

8   WHAT TYPE OF HULL IS DESIGNED TO CUT THROUGH THE WATER RATHER THAN GLIDING ON TOP OF IT?

A   Displacement hull
B   Planing hull
C   Pontoon hull
D   Round-bottom hull

9   IF A BOATER IS LESS THAN 12 YEARS OF AGE AND UNSUPERVISED, WHAT SIZE OF ENGINE CAN HE/SHE LEGALLY OPERATE?

A   25 hp
B   10 hp or less
C   25 hp or less
D   40 hp or less

10   WHICH OF THE FOLLOWING IS THE CORRECT DEFINITION OF A BOAT'S 'HULL'?

A   The portion of the pleasure craft in the water
B   The portion of the pleasure craft both in and above the water
C   The body of the pleasure craft excluding masts, sails, rigging, equipment or machinery
D   The body of the pleasure craft excluding machinery

module 2
RULES, REGULATIONS & EQUIPMENT

The main rules that recreational boaters in Canada must follow are contained in the *Canada Shipping Act 2001* and the *Criminal Code of Canada*. As these laws will change from time to time, it is your responsibility to stay up-to-date on new requirements.

Canada's marine acts, regulations and code are law, and apply **to all boat operators in Canada** (both residents and visitors). You may face fines, penalties or imprisonment if you violate these laws. When travelling abroad you are required to obey the laws of the host country.

The Royal Canadian Mounted Police (RCMP), provincial and municipal police forces and other local authorities enforce Canada's boating laws. **Law enforcement officers may inspect your boat and monitor your activities at any time to ensure that you are in compliance with Canada's boating laws.**

CANADA SHIPPING ACT 2001

The *Canada Shipping Act 2001* establishes a framework of rules and regulations and is the **'umbrella' act under which all boating regulations are developed in Canada.** It incorporates international and federal laws and regulates all boats operating on Canada's waterways.

SMALL VESSEL REGULATIONS

The *Small Vessel Regulations* are part of the *Canada Shipping Act 2001* and outline the minimum mandatory safety equipment that must be aboard your boat. The *Small Vessel Regulations* also outline safety precautions, maintenance procedures to follow before and while boating, boat registration and licensing, and construction standards for building a boat.

CRIMINAL CODE OF CANADA

The *Criminal Code of Canada* enables law enforcement authorities to charge boat operators for criminal offences. The *Criminal Code of Canada*:

- Requires a pleasure craft operator to stop and assist another boat when he/she is in distress, so long as it does not place themselves, their boat or their passengers in a dangerous position

- Requires that a person other than the operator (a spotter) keep watch of any person being towed (like a water-skier)
- Prohibits the towing of water-skiers from one hour after sunset until sunrise
- Prohibits boats from being operated in a manner that is dangerous to the public
- Prohibits false emergency signals or messages
- Prohibits operators from interfering with marine signals and navigation aids
- Prohibits the operation of a boat that is in 'unseaworthy' (poor or unsafe) condition
- Prohibits the operation of a boat while under the influence of drugs, alcohol or controlled substances
- Prohibits the operation of a boat while disqualified or prohibited from boat operation

SAFE BOATING TIPS

01 The offence 'Careless Operation of a Vessel' is part of the *Small Vessel Regulations*. This means no person shall operate a vessel in a careless manner, without proper care and attention or without reasonable consideration for other persons.

02 The *Canada Shipping Act 2001* requires every boat operator to help other boaters who are in distress or found at sea and in danger of being lost, so long as it does not put themselves, their passengers or their own boat at risk.

Unfortunately, boating under the influence is still a significant issue on Canadian waterways. In fact, boating under the influence of **alcohol and/or drugs is still a factor in approximately 40% of boating-related accidents and deaths in Canada.**

In some provinces, any boat operator found guilty of alcohol impairment will lose their motor vehicle driver's license for up to one year. Additionally, the rules vary in each province for when alcohol can be consumed by boat passengers and how alcohol can be transported on a boat.

BOATING AND ALCOHOL: THE LAWS

The *Criminal Code of Canada,* prohibits the following:

- Operating a boat anywhere in Canada while under the influence of alcohol and/or drugs
- Operating a boat in Canada with a **blood alcohol concentration (BAC) in excess of 80 mg**
- Failing or refusing to comply with a demand from an enforcement officer to submit a blood sample

If you drink—don't drive. The same applies whether you're driving a car, a boat or any other type of motorized vehicle. Consuming alcohol, drugs or other controlled substances will not only put your own life at risk, but will also risk the lives of your fellow boaters.

UNLOCK INTERACTIVE CONTENT

Scan this page

More info, including the alcohol laws in your province.

THE NEGATIVE EFFECTS OF BOATING AND ALCOHOL

BOATER FATIGUE:

This negative effect is caused by a combination of the hot sun, wind, noise, vibration and motion of the boat. These factors can quadruple the effects of alcohol on boaters. What's more, alcohol also slows your swallowing and breathing reflexes, making you more likely to drown if you fall overboard.

DEHYDRATION:

Heat and sun can cause dehydration as the body tries to cool itself by sweating. If you're dehydrated, you will feel the effects of alcohol more quickly. Even mildly dehydrated people will absorb alcohol more quickly into their system and will have a higher blood alcohol concentration than a non-dehydrated person. Dehydration causes the body to lose fluids, which can lead to stomach cramps while attempting to swim and stay above water.

OTHER NEGATIVE EFFECTS OF ALCOHOL INCLUDE:

- **Diminished judgment** and ability to process information—alcohol will make you less attentive
- **Slower reaction** and reflex response times
- **Reduced motor skills**, peripheral vision and balance, putting you at greater risk of falling overboard

- **Poor depth perception**, vision and focus
- **Inner ear disturbances**, which makes it harder to distinguish the water surface if you fall in
- **Accelerated hypothermia**, since alcohol lowers the body's resistance to cold

SAFE BOATING TIP
Consuming alcohol and not wearing a life jacket or PFD can be a deadly combination.

WHAT IS A COMPLIANCE NOTICE?

The *Small Vessel Regulations* require all pleasure craft that are less than 24 m in length and that are, or can be, fitted with a motor, **to have a Compliance Notice** (boats longer than 24 m in length are exempt from this requirement). This metal label is attached to your boat's hull and it should be visible from the operator's seat.

INBOARD/STERN-DRIVE UNDER 6M

PLEASURE CRAFT OVER 6M

OUTBOARD CRAFT UNDER 6M

WHAT INFORMATION IS ON A COMPLIANCE NOTICE?

Compliance Notices for boats **less than 6 meters** in length provide 3 important pieces of information:

1. **Maximum number of adults:**
The maximum number of adult persons that your boat can safely carry.

2. **Recommended gross load capacity:**
The maximum weight your boat is designed to carry **including persons, gear, equipment, supplies, fuel and motor assembly.**

3. **Recommended safe limits of engine power:** The maximum limit of horsepower (engine size) based on the boat's gross load capacity.

The Compliance Notice sets a maximum limit for each of these capacities based on safe operation in fair weather conditions. Be aware of the limitations and handling characteristics of your boat and NEVER overload it.

HULL IDENTIFICATION NUMBER

All pleasure craft made in Canada, or imported into Canada after August 1, 1981 (with or without a motor), must have a Hull Identification Number (HIN).

A HIN helps to find lost or stolen boats and identify boats that are subject to a recall. The HIN must be permanently marked on the outside upper starboard corner of the transom, or as close to that area as possible. The HIN is 12 digits long and no character of the HIN can be less than 6 mm (1/4") in height and width.

PLEASURE CRAFT LICENSE

A Pleasure Craft License is a document that contains a set of ID numbers that must be displayed on your boat for identification purposes. A Pleasure Craft License is different than Vessel Registration, which provides proof of ownership.

The *Small Vessel Regulations* require **all boats** that are mostly operated or kept in Canada of all sizes with a propulsion motor of 10 hp (7.5 KW) or more to have a **Pleasure Craft License** (unless they are registered). If your boat is already licensed, make sure that your contact information is up-to-date. You can obtain a 10 year license for free from the Pleasure Craft Licensing Centre. A copy of your vessel license must be carried onboard with you during operation.

You must display your Pleasure Craft License number **above the waterline on both sides of the bow,** as far forward as practical, and where it is easy to see. The numbers must be in block letters, at least 7.5 cm (3") high, and must contrast with the colour of the background.

VESSEL REGISTRATION

Vessel Registration is different from Vessel Licensing in that it provides proof of ownership (legal title), a unique name and official number for your boat and the right to use your boat as security for a marine mortgage. There are costs involved but if you plan on travelling in international waters, it is recommended.

In order to register your boat you will be required to:

- Select at least 3 names for your boat (only one will be approved)
- Pay a registration fee
- Complete an application for registry
- Produce evidence of ownership/title and statement of qualification for vessel registration
- Have your boat measured for tonnage

For more information about Pleasure Craft Licensing and Registration visit **www.boatingsafety.gc.ca** or call 1-800-267-6687

HOW TO TRANSFER BOAT OWNERSHIP

If selling a boat, you must immediately transfer the ownership by signing the reverse side of your Pleasure Craft License. Then, you must provide it to the new owner, who must complete and sign the reverse side of the Pleasure Craft License and submit it to Transport Canada's Pleasure Craft Licensing Centre for transfer within 90 days. An owner may operate the boat for 90 days after the date of change of name or address, if documents establishing the date of change of name or address are onboard.

FOR SALE
1987 wavejumper

WHAT ARE MY RESPONSIBILITIES?

As a boat operator in Canada you are legally responsible for equipping yourself, your passengers and your boat with the right equipment. You are also responsible for operating your boat in a safe and courteous manner and for ensuring the safety of your passengers and other boaters on the water. Failure to do so could result in fines and penalties.

USING COMMON COURTESY

You are **required by law** to operate your boat in a **safe** and **courteous** manner. Use common sense, take responsibility for your actions and consider the following factors every time you operate your boat:

- Your distance from shore
- Water and wind speed conditions
- Visibility conditions
- Local hazards and obstructions
- The amount of boat traffic in the vicinity
- Your boat's handling characteristics and capabilities
- Your level of skill and experience
- Posted speed limits

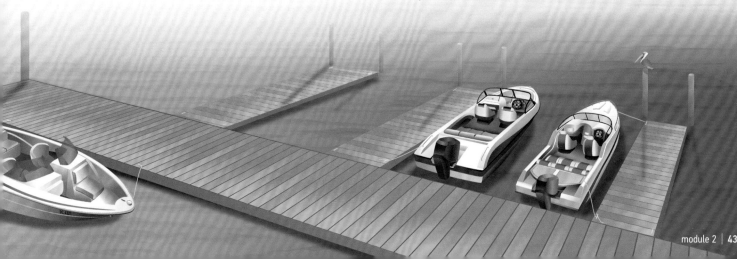

VESSEL OPERATION RESTRICTION REGULATIONS

Local restrictions have been placed on some Canadian waterways to promote public safety. Some of these regulations include a ban on motorized boats, maximum engine power limits, speed limits and a ban on recreational towing activities. The regulations also limit where certain types of boats may or may not be permitted to operate in Canada. Operators are required to comply with these regulations and should check locally for more information.

WILL YOU BE LENDING YOUR BOAT OR PWC?

Understand that if you plan on lending your watercraft to a friend, both you (the owner) and the person borrowing your boat (the operator) are responsible for the boat. You should ensure that the operator:

- Has obtained a Pleasure Craft Operator Card
- Understands Canada's boating laws and regulations and is a responsible person
- Wears an approved life jacket or PFD
- Understands navigation and right-of-way rules
- Understands the handling characteristics of your craft
- Knows about the location of local hazards or obstructions
- Knows the location of safety equipment on your craft and how to use it

SAFE BOATING TIP

The *Vessel Operation Restriction Regulations* limit where certain types of boats are restricted from operating or where special conditions apply (like swimming areas).

SAFETY EQUIPMENT

Always have the right equipment onboard–it's one of the most important things you can do to ensure you are boating safely and it's the law. **You are violating the *Small Vessel Regulations* if you operate a pleasure craft that does not have the required safety equipment onboard, or if it is not in good working order.** The same law applies if you loan your boat. Show your passengers how to use the safety equipment so that everyone is prepared in the event of an emergency. Be sure to check the safety equipment before and after every trip to ensure it will work properly when needed.

The *Small Vessel Regulations* require that certain safety equipment be carried onboard at all times. The type of equipment required varies according to the **type and length of your boat**.

The *Small Vessel Regulations* require your safety equipment to be:

- In good working order
- Regularly maintained
- Replaced in accordance with the manufacturer's instructions
- Readily accessible for immediate use

THERE ARE FOUR TYPES OF BOATING SAFETY EQUIPMENT REQUIRED IN CANADA:

> **01 PERSONAL SAFETY EQUIPMENT**

> **02 BOAT SAFETY EQUIPMENT**

> **03 DISTRESS EQUIPMENT**

> **04 NAVIGATION EQUIPMENT**

›01 PERSONAL SAFETY EQUIPMENT

Your personal safety equipment must be carried onboard at all times. This includes:

- Life jackets and personal flotation devices (PFDs)
- Buoyant heaving line

APPROVED FLOTATION DEVICES

Wearing a Canadian-approved, properly fitted flotation device will greatly reduce the risk of accidental drowning. In fact, statistics show that most small craft operators who drown are often within sight of a potential rescuer and would likely have been saved had they just remained afloat a few moments longer.

There are 3 main types of Canadian-approved flotation devices:

- Life jackets
- Personal flotation devices (PFDs)
- Inflatable PFDs

HOW WILL I KNOW IF MY FLOTATION DEVICE IS CANADIAN-APPROVED?

Canadian-approved flotation devices bear a label or stamp indicating approval by Transport Canada or by the Canadian Coast Guard. Be aware that not all PFDs are Canadian-approved. Always check the label.

The approval status of a life jacket or PFD is void if it has been damaged, altered, repaired or if the label or stamp indicating approval is illegible. If ripped or damaged, replace your flotation device immediately.

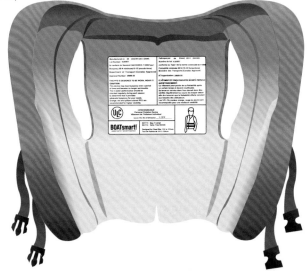

SAFE BOATING TIP

More than 90 percent of all persons who drown while boating were not wearing a life jacket or PFD.

Remember: your flotation device only works if you wear it! Life jackets and PFDs should be worn by ALL boaters in and around water and not just when operating or riding in a boat.

LIFE JACKETS

Life jackets can be found in both 'Standard' and 'Small Vessel' styles and are available in both youth and adult sizes. They are red, orange or yellow in colour, feature a 'keyhole' or 'vest' design and are typically bulkier and more uncomfortable than PFDs. Manufactured with increased flotation in the front of the jacket, **life jackets are designed to turn an unconscious person face up** in the water.

There are a few different types of life jackets:

- SOLAS (SAFETY OF LIFE AT SEA) life jackets offer the best performance and will **turn an unconscious person face up** in seconds

- STANDARD LIFE JACKETS feature a high degree of buoyancy and will **turn an unconscious person face up** but are typically uncomfortable

- SMALL VESSEL LIFE JACKETS are also **designed to turn an unconscious person face up,** but are not as buoyant and have less turning ability

Life jackets should fit slightly loose in order to allow water under the front of the jacket so that it can function properly. All zippers, fasteners, buckles and straps should be adjusted to ensure a proper fit. Although you can choose between life jackets and PFDs, keep in mind that **life jackets offer a higher level of protection.**

SOLAS
LIFE JACKET

STANDARD
LIFE JACKET

SMALL VESSEL
LIFE JACKET

PERSONAL FLOTATION DEVICES (PFDS)

Personal Flotation Devices (PFDs) are more comfortable and less restrictive than life jackets. **PFDs are designed to keep a person afloat but are NOT designed to turn an unconscious person face up** in the water.

PFDs come in keyhole, vest, coat and coverall designs. Child, youth and adult sizes are available and should be fitted to the size of the person wearing the device. PFDs should fit snugly but not restrict the free movement of arms and legs.

INFLATABLE PFDS

Inflatable PFDs have a carbon dioxide cartridge that is used to inflate the PFD. Once inflated, the PFD is able to keep the person afloat. They are very comfortable and compact to wear and come in various styles including waist pouches, vests and those that automatically inflate, versus more basic styles that require manual inflation.

THE RULES FOR INFLATABLE PFDS:

- **Only approved for use by persons 16 years or older** that weigh more than 36 kilograms
- Must be **worn at all times while on deck or in the cockpit of an open boat**
- Must be **readily available to persons below deck** on boats equipped with cabins
- Are not approved for use on **PWCs or during white water activities**

BOATsmart!

UNLOCK INTERACTIVE CONTENT

Scan this page

Check out an Inflatable PFD in action!

MAKING THE RIGHT CHOICE

When choosing a life jacket or PFD, you should consider the following:

- Check the label or stamp to confirm the flotation device is Canadian-approved
- Choose one that suits the type of boating activities you will be doing. Will you be wakeboarding? Operating a PWC? Fishing?
- Verify that the life jacket or PFD is appropriate for your size and weight (if a boater falls overboard when wearing a PFD that is too small, **it may not support the weight of that person**)
- Check that it fits snugly but allows for freedom of movement
- If purchasing a life jacket or PFD for another person, ensure that it will fit that person

SAFE BOATING TIP

If you are in a smaller, open boat (such as a small fishing boat), other boaters may find it difficult to see you. Choosing a brightly-coloured flotation device will help to make you more visible to others.

S

Chest Size –
87 cm to 97 cm
Weight –
99 lbs. – 154 lbs.

M

Chest Size –
96 cm to 107 cm
Weight –
132 lbs. – 198 lbs.

L

Chest Size –
107 cm to 117 cm
Weight –
176 lbs - 242 lbs.

CHILDREN'S LIFE JACKETS AND PFDS

Many life jackets, although certified for use, may not properly protect a child. Choose a life jacket or PFD that has been specifically designed for use by children to ensure their safety.

A CHILDREN'S LIFE JACKET OR PFD SHOULD HAVE THE FOLLOWING:

- A label or stamp indicating that it is Canadian-approved
- An extra large collar to support the child's head
- A safety strap that fastens between the legs to prevent the jacket from slipping over the child's head
- A grab strap located on the collar
- Reflective material and a safety whistle

Children should be encouraged to wear a life jacket or PFD at all times – both on the boat and when they are near the water. Be sure that children understand how to properly fit and use their life jacket or PFD and never consider a flotation device to be a substitute for adult supervision.

The life jacket or PFD should always properly fit the child. Never try to make do with a flotation device and never purchase a larger size in the hope that the child will 'grow into it'.

TESTING LIFE JACKETS AND PFDS

Life jackets and PFDs should be **tested for buoyancy** at the start of each season and on a regular basis throughout the season. Even if they are new!

Children should also test their life jackets or PFDs to ensure proper fit and buoyancy. Have your child follow the same procedures outlined below in a controlled environment under parental supervision.

STEP 1

Put on and properly fit the life jacket or PFD. Wade into chest deep water.

STEP 2

Bend your knees and float onto your back.

STEP 3

Ensure the life jacket or PFD keeps your chin above the water and permits proper breathing.

MAINTAINING YOUR LIFE JACKETS AND PFDS

Life jackets and PFDs are designed to save lives, but in order for them to do their job, you have to do yours. It is each boater's responsibility to maintain and care for their flotation device on a regular basis.

HOW TO CARE FOR YOUR LIFE JACKET OR PFD:

- **Never use them as cushions, bumpers or fenders**—they may become damaged and less effective
- They should be **air-dried out of direct sunlight** and away from a direct heat source
- When not in use they should be stowed onboard your boat in a **dry, well-ventilated area**
- Store them in an **easily accessible** location and never in the proximity of gasoline or chemicals
- **Inspect your life jackets and PFDs regularly**—if ripped or damaged, they should be replaced immediately
- Remember that inflatable PFDs require more technology, which means they **must be maintained more often** than the other types of life jackets and PFDs (the owner's manual will provide all the additional information you need)

HOW TO CLEAN A LIFE JACKET OR PFD:

1. Use **mild soap and water**
2. Rinse thoroughly
3. Never dry-clean or use strong detergents, gasoline or chemicals/solvents
4. Air dry out of direct sunlight and away from direct heat sources

HOW TO PUT ON A FLOTATION DEVICE IN THE WATER

Find a supervised area in which to practice the following procedure:

SAFE BOATING TIP

It can be extremely difficult to put on a flotation device while in the water. It is highly recommended that you **wear a life jacket or PFD at all times while onboard your boat.**

01

02

03

04

STEP 1

Spread the flotation device open with the inside facing up and out of the water and the neck facing towards you.

STEP 2

Extend your arms through the arm openings.

STEP 3

Lift your arms above your head, lie backwards and pull the flotation device around your upper body.

STEP 4

Fasten the zipper, straps, buckles and/or ties to ensure a snug fit.

BUOYANT HEAVING LINE

A buoyant heaving line is **designed to be thrown overboard to rescue a person from the water.** Some heaving lines are light and can be more difficult to throw long distances. Using a buoyant heaving line equipped with a throw container (a weighted plastic shell or bag at one end) will enable you to throw with less difficulty.

The *Small Vessel Regulations* require that buoyant heaving lines be:

- At least **15 m in length for all pleasure craft under 24 m in length**
- Readily accessible in case of emergency

EMERGENCY KIT

Although not required, boat operators are encouraged to carry an emergency kit on their boat at all times. The kit should be stored in a watertight plastic bag and should include:

- Emergency food and drinking water
- A first aid kit
- Waterproof matches
- A waterproof flashlight
- A knife
- A whistle
- Dry clothing

0 m   24 m

0 m   15 m

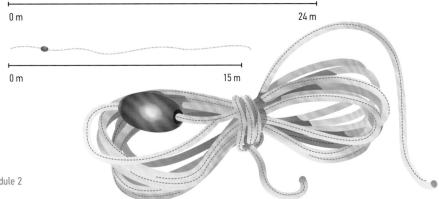

> 02 BOAT SAFETY EQUIPMENT

You are required to carry boat safety equipment at all times. The safety equipment must be maintained and kept in good working order because it can be the difference between life and death in an emergency situation. Different sizes and types of boats are required to carry different equipment (refer to Appendix A at the end of this module for a complete list of the required equipment).

BOAT SAFETY EQUIPMENT INCLUDES:

- Bailing devices
- Life buoy
- Manual and electric bilge pumps
- Manual propelling devices (oars/paddles)
- Axe
- Repair kit
- Re-boarding device (ladder)
- Fire extinguisher
- Anchor

SAFE BOATING TIP

It's a good idea to store all your safety equipment in a duffle bag or container. Keeping it readily accessible and available ensures you'll find it when you need it most!

BAILING DEVICE

A bailing device is used to remove water from inside a boat. *The Small Vessel Regulations* require bailers to:

- Be made of metal or plastic
- Have a volume of at least 750 ml and an opening that is at least 65 cm2 in area

BUCKETS

Buckets can be used to fight fires and dispel water from your boat.

- Motorized boats over 12 m and up to 24 m in length are required to carry two buckets with a 10L minimum capacity
- Motorized boats over 24 m in length are required to carry four buckets with a 10L minimum capacity

LIFE BUOY

A life buoy (sometimes called a life ring) is a device that can be used to rescue a person who has fallen overboard. To be approved, a life buoy must have no tears, perforations or rot and the gridlines must be secure and in good condition.

A life buoy is required to:

- Be circular in shape
- Have an outside **diameter of either 610 mm or 762 mm**
- Carry a sticker indicating that it has been approved by Transport Canada
- Be attached to a **line of at least 15 m in length and appropriate for the size of your vessel**

BILGE PUMPS

MANUAL BILGE PUMPS

If using a manual bilge pump to dispel water from the boat, you must ensure the discharge hose is long enough to reach from the bilge to over the side of your boat.

ELECTRIC BILGE PUMPS

Electric bilge pumps are designed to remove water from the hull of a vessel. Some electric bilge pumps will turn on automatically if the water level in the bilge begins to rise. Boats fitted with electric bilge pumps are recommended to carry a manual pump or bailing device as a back-up in case of mechanical failure.

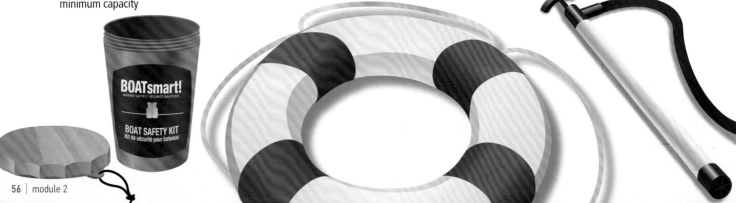

MANUAL PROPELLING DEVICE

Manual propelling devices can be used to manoeuver your boat in the case of a breakdown. Most boats are required to carry paddles or oars with oar locks. If operating a boat less than 8 m in length, you may use an anchor with a minimum of 15 m of rope, cable or chain in place of a manual propelling device.

AXE

Those operating large boats (longer than 12 m in length) must carry one axe onboard at all times. An axe must be protected from the elements and kept in an easily accessible location. It can be used to chop into a wall that is concealing open flames or to cut a towline in an emergency.

REPAIR KIT

Although not mandatory equipment, boaters should always carry a repair kit that includes essential tools and spare parts. Tapered wooden plugs, underwater sealing compounds, patch kits and duct tape can all be used to help stop hull leaks.

RE-BOARDING EQUIPMENT

A re-boarding device, such as a transom or swim platform ladder appropriate to the size of the vessel, is designed to allow easy re-boarding of your boat from the water. *The Small Vessel Regulations* require that all boats carry an effective re-boarding device **if the freeboard of the boat is greater than 0.5 m.** A re-boarding device cannot be part of the propulsion unit.

UNLOCK INTERACTIVE CONTENT

Scan this page

See how equipment works and where you can buy it online.

FIRE EXTINGUISHER

Fire extinguishers are **required** onboard any boats with a motor and any one of the following:

- Closed compartments where portable fuel tanks may be stored
- Closed living and cooking spaces
- Permanently installed fuel tanks
- Enclosed engine compartments

Boaters should mount a fire extinguisher in an easily accessible location where it can be quickly retrieved in case of emergency. Though not required for all motorboats, it is highly recommended that every operator in a motorized boat carry a fire extinguisher.

EXTINGUISHER RATING SYSTEM:

Fire extinguishers are rated using a system of letters and numbers:

- CLASS A: Designed for use on combustible solid materials such as wood and paper
- CLASS B: Designed for use on combustible liquid fires including gas, oil and grease
- CLASS C: Designed for use on electrical fires

A   B   C

The number identifies the amount of agent (material that puts out the fire) that is inside the extinguisher. The higher the number, the greater the amount of fire-fighting agent in the device. For example, a Class 3 extinguisher can extinguish a larger fire than a Class 2 extinguisher.

The *Small Vessel Regulations* **require that Class BC extinguishers be used on boats in Canada. However, the use of a Class ABC fire extinguisher is recommended.** Ensure that the fire extinguisher you choose meets the requirements for the size and type of your boat. Remember, even if your boat is equipped with an automatic extinguishing system, you still must carry portable fire extinguishers.

SAFE BOATING TIP

Fire extinguishers must be approved by the Underwriters Laboratories of Canada (ULC), the Underwriters Laboratory (UL), or the U.S. Coast Guard (USCG).

ANCHOR

An anchor can be used during an engine failure emergency or during bad weather to keep you from drifting towards obstacles. **If operating a boat 9 m in length or longer you are required to carry an anchor.** The *Small Vessel Regulations* also require that **an anchor be fitted with at least 15, 30 or 50 m of cable, rope or chain in any combination** (the length depends on your boat).

ANCHOR TYPES:

- **'FISHERMAN'** anchors are a non-burying type with one arm that penetrates the bottom (best used for rocky bottoms)
- **'FLUKE'** anchors (or 'Danforth' anchors) have pointed flukes that dig into the ground (best used for grass and mud)
- **'PLOUGH'** anchors function like a farmer's plough and can be harder to set (best used with rocky bottoms)
- **'BRUCE' OR 'CLAW'** anchors are popular for small boats because they set easily and tend to maintain their hold during changes in wind and tide (best used in most waterway bottoms)

Choosing the right anchor depends on the size and weight of your boat and the characteristics of the waterway bottom (i.e. sand, rock or mud). Larger anchors are recommended for adverse conditions and those equipped with a shackle pin should have a locking device.

REMEMBER:
Securely fasten the end of your anchor line to the bow of your boat and securely attach the outboard end of the anchor line to the anchor!

FLUKE

BRUCE/CLAW

PLOUGH

FISHERMAN

› 03 DISTRESS EQUIPMENT

Certain distress equipment is required to be carried onboard pleasure craft at all times. This is so you have it in the event of an emergency situation like a collision, a medical emergency or a mechanical breakdown. Situations like these, where you may require the use of a flare, are often unexpected, but if they happen to you, you'll be happy to have the distress equipment when you need it most.

WATERTIGHT FLASHLIGHT

Most craft are required to carry one watertight flashlight onboard at all times. In an emergency, a flashlight can be used for illumination or to send a distress signal. To be approved, **the batteries must be in good condition**. A watertight flashlight qualifies as navigation lights on non-powered vessels less than 7 m in length.

SAFE BOATING TIP

You can signal your need for help by flashing **S.O.S.: three short flashes, then three long flashes, followed by three short flashes.**

FLARES

Flares and pyrotechnic devices are used to signal distress and need of assistance. They should always be stored in a watertight container and located in a cool, dry, accessible area. You may be required to carry certain types of flares onboard your boat depending on:

- The size and type of boat
- The body of water on which you are operating

For example:

- You are required to carry flares if operating on any ocean or if operating on a waterway where you may be further than one nautical mile from shore
- You are not required to carry flares if you are operating on a river, canal or lake on which at no time your boat can be more than one nautical mile from shore

TYPES OF APPROVED FLARES

There are four types of flares approved to signal your need for help:

TYPE A: PARACHUTE FLARE

- Easily seen from water, land and air
- Must emit a red light

TYPE B: MULTI-STAR FLARE

- Easily seen from water, land and air
- Must emit a red light

TYPE C: HAND-HELD FLARE

- Not as easily seen from afar but effective for pinpointing your position
- Must emit a red light

TYPE D: SMOKE FLARE

- Highly visible during daylight hours
- Must give off orange smoke

USING FLARES

All flares and pyrotechnic distress signals must be approved for use by Transport Canada and are valid for only four years from their date of manufacture. Flares or other pyrotechnic devices should always be used with caution and kept out of the reach of children. Always follow the manufacturer's instructions located on the packaging or casing before using a flare.

It is illegal to test or discharge a flare if it is not being used for an emergency situation and you should only dispose of flares in an approved manner. Contact your manufacturer, local law enforcement agency, fire department or the Canadian Coast Guard for proper disposal procedures.

SAFE BOATING TIP

Remember: when operating your boat, you are required to maintain a look-out for signals that indicate a fellow boater is in distress or in need of assistance.

> 04 NAVIGATION EQUIPMENT

Navigation equipment (like sound signals and navigation lights) are required on all boats in Canada. Their purpose is to attract the attention of other boaters and to aid with navigation on the water.

SOUND-SIGNALLING DEVICES AND APPLIANCES

The *Small Vessel Regulations* require that all boats carry some form of sound-signalling device, such as a whistle or horn. The requirement depends on your type and size of boat. Approved sound-signalling devices and appliances must be audible for a minimum of 0.93 km.

Sound-signalling devices are used to signal distress or your need of assistance, to alert other boats of your position in poor visibility and for navigation purposes.

Types of sound-signalling devices include:

- Mechanical (floatless) whistle
- Horn
- Portable compressed air horns
- Bell – required if your boat is greater than 20 metres

SAFE BOATING TIP

You should attach a Marine Blast Whistle to your life jacket or PFD so that you'll be able to signal for help if you become stranded in the water.

NAVIGATION LIGHTS

You are required to display your navigation lights **between sunset and sunrise**. Navigation lights must also be exhibited **during periods of reduced visibility** such as fog or heavy rain conditions.

If operating a non-powered craft that does not have fixed navigation lights, then you must have a watertight flashlight or lantern that can emit a white light.

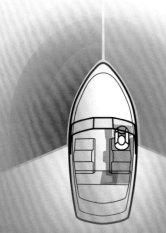

RADAR REFLECTOR

A radar reflector is a metallic device that is used to identify the position of your boat to other vessels equipped with radar. Radar reflectors are required for boats under 20 m and boats that are built of mostly non-metallic materials. The radar reflector should be suspended above all equipment and as high as possible.

A radar reflector is not required if:

- It is impractical to mount on your boat
- Traffic conditions are limited and no other vessels use radar
- You are operating during daylight hours in good weather conditions
- The use of radar reflector is not essential for safe operation of your craft

HUMAN-POWERED BOATS

PERSONAL SAFETY EQUIPMENT

1 Canadian-approved PFD or life jacket for each person onboard

1 buoyant heaving line at least 15m long

1 reboarding device if freeboard is greater than 0.5m

BOAT SAFETY EQUIPMENT

1 bailer or manual bilge pump or bilge-pumping arrangements***

NAVIGATION EQUIPMENT

1 sound-signalling device or appliance

1 magnetic compass*

Navigation lights**

1 radar reflector (see page 59)

DISTRESS EQUIPMENT

If boat is over 6m:

1 watertight flashlight

6 flares of type A, B or C

SAILBOARDS & KITEBOARDS

PERSONAL SAFETY EQUIPMENT

1 Canadian-approved PFD or life jacket for each person onboard

1 buoyant heaving line at least 15m long

1 reboarding device if freeboard is greater than 0.5m

BOAT SAFETY EQUIPMENT

1 manual propelling device or 1 anchor and at least 15m of cable, rope or chain in any combination

1 bailer or manual bilge pump***

NAVIGATION EQUIPMENT

1 sound-signalling device or appliance

1 magnetic compass*

Navigation lights**

1 radar reflector (see page 59)

DISTRESS EQUIPMENT

None

All items marked in blue are not required if you are operating a paddleboat, watercycle or sealed-hull sit on top kayak and everyone onboard is wearing a PFD or life jacket

Items marked in red are not required if everyone onboard is wearing a PFD or life jacket

* Not required if the boat is 8m or less and operated within sight of navigation marks

**Only required if the boat is operated after sunset, before sunrise or in periods of restricted visibility

***Not required for a boat that cannot hold enough water to make it capsize, or a boat that has watertight compartments that are sealed and not readily accessible

PERSONAL WATERCRAFT (PWCs)

PERSONAL SAFETY EQUIPMENT

1 Canadian-approved PFD or life jacket for each person onboard

1 buoyant heaving line at least 15m long

1 reboarding device if freeboard is greater than 0.5m

BOAT SAFETY EQUIPMENT

1 manual propelling device or 1 anchor and at least 15m of cable, rope or chain in any combination

1 bailer or manual bilge pump***

1 fire extinguisher (5BC)

NAVIGATION EQUIPMENT

1 sound-signalling device or appliance

1 magnetic compass*

Navigation lights**

1 radar reflector (see page 59)

DISTRESS EQUIPMENT

1 watertight flashlight or 3 flares of type A, B or C

SAIL & POWERED CRAFT (UP TO 6M IN LENGTH)

PERSONAL SAFETY EQUIPMENT

1 Canadian-approved PFD or life jacket for each person onboard

1 buoyant heaving line at least 15m long

1 reboarding device if freeboard is greater than 0.5m

BOAT SAFETY EQUIPMENT

1 manual propelling device or 1 anchor and at least 15m of cable, rope or chain in any combination

1 bailer or manual bilge pump***

1 fire extinguisher (5BC) if equipped with a motor, a fixed fuel tank of any size, or any fuel-burning, cooking, heating or refrigerator appliance

NAVIGATION EQUIPMENT

1 sound-signalling device or appliance

1 magnetic compass*

Navigation lights**

1 radar reflector (see page 59)

DISTRESS EQUIPMENT

If the boat is equipped with a motor:

1 watertight flashlight or 3 flares of type A, B or C

Items marked in red are not required if everyone onboard is wearing a PFD or life jacket

* Not required if the boat is 8m or less and operated within sight of navigation marks

**Only required if the boat is operated after sunset, before sunrise or in periods of restricted visibility

***Not required for a boat that cannot hold enough water to make it capsize, or a boat that has watertight compartments that are sealed and not readily accessible

SAIL & POWERED CRAFT (OVER 6M AND UP TO 9M IN LENGTH)

PERSONAL SAFETY EQUIPMENT

1 Canadian-approved PFD or life jacket for each person onboard

1 buoyant heaving line at least 15m long or

1 life buoy attached to a buoyant line at least 15m long

1 reboarding device if freeboard is greater than 0.5m

BOAT SAFETY EQUIPMENT

1 manual propelling device or 1 anchor and at least 15m of cable, rope or chain in any combination

1 bailer or manual bilge pump***

1 fire extinguisher (5BC) if equipped with a motor

1 fire extinguisher (5BC) if equipped with any fuel-burning, cooking, heating or refrigerator appliance

NAVIGATION EQUIPMENT

1 sound-signalling device or appliance

1 magnetic compass*

Navigation lights**

1 radar reflector (see page 59)

DISTRESS EQUIPMENT

1 watertight flashlight

6 flares of type A, B or C

SAIL & POWERED CRAFT (OVER 9M AND UP TO 12M IN LENGTH)

PERSONAL SAFETY EQUIPMENT

1 Canadian-approved PFD or life jacket for each person onboard

1 buoyant heaving line at least 15m long

1 life buoy attached to a buoyant line at least 15m long

A reboarding device if freeboard is greater than 0.5m

BOAT SAFETY EQUIPMENT

1 anchor and at least 30m of cable, rope or chain in any combination

1 manual bilge pump*** or bilge pumping arrangements

1 fire extinguisher (10BC) if equipped with a motor

1 fire extinguisher (10BC) if equipped with any fuel-burning, cooking, heating or refrigerator appliance

NAVIGATION EQUIPMENT

1 sound-signalling device or appliance

1 magnetic compass*

Navigation lights**

1 radar reflector (see page 59)

DISTRESS EQUIPMENT

1 watertight flashlight

12 flares of type A, B, C or D (not more than 6 of Type D)

* Not required if the boat is 8m or less and operated within sight of navigation marks

**Only required if the boat is operated after sunset, before sunrise or in periods of restricted visibility

***Not required for a boat that cannot hold enough water to make it capsize, or a boat that has watertight compartments that are sealed and not readily accessible

SAIL & POWERED CRAFT (OVER 12M AND UP TO 24M IN LENGTH)

PERSONAL SAFETY EQUIPMENT

1 Canadian-approved PFD or life jacket for each person onboard

1 buoyant heaving line at least 15m long

1 life buoy equipped with a self-igniting light or attached to a buoyant line at least 15m long

A reboarding device if freeboard is greater than 0.5m

BOAT SAFETY EQUIPMENT

1 anchor and at least 50m of cable, rope or chain in any combination

Bilge pumping arrangements

1 axe

2 buckets (each with a capacity of at least 10 L)

1 fire extinguisher (10BC) at the entrance to:
- any space with a fuel-burning, cooking, heating or refrigerator appliance
- any accommodation space
- the machinery space

NAVIGATION EQUIPMENT

2 sound-signalling devices or appliances (a vessel of 20m or more in length must have a bell in addition to a whistle)

Navigation lights

1 magnetic compass that meets the Navigation Safety Regulations

1 radar reflector (see page 59)

DISTRESS EQUIPMENT

1 watertight flashlight

12 flares Type A, B, C or D (not more than 6 of Type D)

SAIL & POWERED CRAFT(OVER 24 M IN LENGTH)

PERSONAL SAFETY EQUIPMENT

1 Canadian-approved PFD or life jacket for each person onboard

1 buoyant heaving line at least 30m long

2 SOLAS life buoys, of which 1 is attached to 30m of buoyant heaving line and 1 must have a self igniting light

1 lifting harness with appropriate rigging

1 reboarding device if freeboard is greater than 0.5m

BOAT SAFETY EQUIPMENT

1 anchor with at least 50m of line, rope or chain in any combination

Bilge pumping arrangements

2 axes

4 buckets (each with a capacity of 10 L)

1 fire extinguisher (10BC) at the entrance to:
- any space with a fuel-burning, cooking, heating or refrigerator appliance
- any accommodation space
- the machinery space

1 power-driven fire pump located outside the machinery space, with 1 fire hose and nozzle that can direct water into any part of the boat

NAVIGATION EQUIPMENT

2 sound-signalling devices or appliances (must have a bell in addition to a whistle)

Navigation lights

1 magnetic compass that meets the Navigation Safety Regulations

1 radar reflector (see page 59)

DISTRESS EQUIPMENT

1 watertight flashlight

12 flares Type A, B, C or D (not more than 6 of Type D)

---

* Not required if the boat is 8m or less and operated within sight of navigation marks

**Only required if the boat is operated after sunset, before sunrise or in periods of restricted visibility

***Not required for a boat that cannot hold enough water to make it capsize, or a boat that has watertight compartments that are sealed and not readily accessible

MODULE 2 SUMMARY

Canadian boating laws and regulations have been implemented to protect the safety of boat operators and to establish operating and navigation standards to which **all boaters** must comply. For in-depth information on Canadian boating rules and regulations, please contact the Office of Boating Safety at 1-800-267-6687.

Always use courtesy and common sense when operating your boat. Always say NO to drinking and boating, always choose to operate at a safe speed and always come to the aid of fellow boaters who need help, so long as you don't put yourself at risk. By operating your boat in a safe and responsible manner, you'll increase safe and enjoyable boating for all.

Having the required safety equipment onboard at all times and knowing how to use it will enable you to respond effectively in emergency situations. Be sure to maintain and store safety equipment properly so it is readily accessible and working properly when you need it. Always wear an approved life jacket or PFD and ensure your passengers do the same.

Remember: Carrying the right safety equipment is not only the law, it can also save your life!

MODULE 2 QUIZ

1 WHY DO BOATS WITH GREATER THAN 0.5 M FREEBOARD REQUIRE AN APPROVED RE-BOARDING DEVICE?

A   To allow easy re-boarding from the water
B   To assist with boarding your vessel at a dock
C   To assist with loading equipment
D   To assist when refueling

2 WHICH LAW, ACT OR REGULATION PROHIBITS BOATERS FROM OPERATING THEIR CRAFT IN A 'CARELESS MANNER'?

A   *Contraventions Act*
B   *Careless Operation of Marine Vessel Regulations*
C   *Vessel Operation Restriction Regulations*
D   *Small Vessel Regulations*

3 WHAT DOES THE MAXIMUM LOAD ON A COMPLIANCE NOTICE REFER TO?

A   The weight of persons, gear, equipment, supplies, fuel and motor assembly
B   The weight of gear and fuel–not including the weight of passengers
C   The weight of the boat during rainy operating conditions
D   The weight of the passengers, gear and equipment–not including the motor

MODULE 2 QUIZ

4   HOW MANY CANADIAN-APPROVED LIFE JACKETS OR PFDS ARE YOU REQUIRED TO CARRY ONBOARD YOUR BOAT?

A   At least one SOLAS type life jacket
B   Two SOLAS types and two regular types
C   One for every person onboard the boat
D   One for every seat on the boat

5   WHICH PLEASURE CRAFT ARE REQUIRED TO CARRY AN ANCHOR?

A   Those over 6 m in length
B   Those 9 m in length or longer
C   Those equipped with an engine
D   Those equipped with sleeping quarters

6   WHICH ACT, CODE OR REGULATION REQUIRES THAT SAFETY EQUIPMENT BE CARRIED ONBOARD AT ALL TIMES?

A   The *Criminal Code of Canada*
B   The *Small Vessel Regulations*
C   The *Boating Restriction Regulations*
D   The *Collision Regulations*

7   DO PERSONAL WATERCRAFT NEED TO BE LICENSED?

A   No
B   Yes
C   Only if used more than 1 nautical mile from shore
D   Only if the engine size exceeds 40 hp

8   THE SMALL VESSEL REGULATIONS REQUIRE THAT CERTAIN PLEASURE CRAFT MUST BE LICENSED, UNLESS THEY ARE REGISTERED. WHICH ARE THEY?

A   All craft over 6 m in length
B   All craft regardless of their size and length
C   All craft that are able to transport passengers
D   All craft powered by 10 hp (7.5 KW) or more

9   WHAT TYPE OF CLEANER OR SOLVENT SHOULD YOU USE TO CLEAN AN APPROVED FLOTATION DEVICE?

A   Gasoline
B   Chemical solvents
C   Mild soap and water
D   Colour safe bleach

10 UNDER WHICH OF THE FOLLOWING CONDITIONS ARE YOU REQUIRED TO HELP OTHER BOATERS IN DISTRESS?

A   Only when it is safe for you to do so and it doesn't put yourself and/or your passengers at risk
B   You are always required to help other boaters in distress
C   Only if your boat is equipped with a VHF radio
D   Only if you have an EPIRB distress beacon onboard

module 3
BEFORE HEADING OUT

MAINTAINING YOUR CRAFT

There's nothing more enjoyable than a day on the water. Don't let it get spoiled by a breakdown. As a responsible boater, you should always plan ahead and properly maintain your vessel and equipment. Inspect your boat regularly, at the beginning of each boating season and **before every boating trip**. Being familiar with basic repairs will help to ensure your safety and the safety of your passengers.

Being properly prepared and maintaining your equipment will also alleviate unnecessary burden on search and rescue organizations such as the Canadian Coast Guard. You'll also save time and money by reducing the chance of costly breakdowns.

REMEMBER:
The *Criminal Code of Canada* requires that you maintain your boat and equipment in seaworthy condition. **It's the law.**

Visit **BoatSmartExam.com**® to download a Pre-Season Maintenance checklist.

Scan to download a BOATsmart!® Pre-Season Maintenance Checklist!

Engine
Oil

BOATsmart! »»

PRE-SEASON MAINTENANCE CHECKLIST

RECOMMENDED INSPECTIONS:

- [ ] CHECK THE HULL AND BILGE FOR ANY DAMAGE INCLUDING CRACKS AND LEAKS
- [ ] CHECK THE CONDITION OF AND OPERATION OF THE OUTDRIVE, INCLUDING:
  - [ ] SHAFTS
  - [ ] PROPELLERS (PROP)
  - [ ] NUTS AND PINS
- [ ] CHECK THE OPERATION AND CONDITION OF ALL SYSTEMS, INCLUDING:
  - [ ] FUEL, ELECTRICAL AND COOLING SYSTEMS
- [ ] CHECK THE CONDITION OF HOSES AND LINES AND REPLACE WORN, BROKEN OR CRACKED LINES
- [ ] CHECK THE CONDITION OF THE THROTTLE CONTROL
- [ ] CHECK ALL ELECTRICAL CONNECTIONS - CLEAN AND TIGHTEN ANY CORRODED OR LOOSE CONNECTIONS
- [ ] CHECK THE CONDITION OF ALL NAVIGATION LIGHTS
- [ ] INSPECT AND CLEAN THE ENGINE'S FLAME ARRESTOR WITH SOAP AND WATER
- [ ] CHECK AND REPLACE ENGINE OIL AND FUEL FILTERS IF NECESSARY
- [ ] WITH ENGINE RUNNING, CHECK THE OPERATION OF ALL GAUGES AND ALTERNATOR FOR CHARGING CAPACITY
- [ ] WITH THE ENGINE RUNNING, CHECK THE OPERATION OF ALL GAUGES AND ALTERNATOR FOR CHARGING CAPACITY
- [ ] CHECK THE CONDITION OF THE BATTERY (A FULLY CHARGED BATTERY SHOULD HOLD IT'S CHARGE FOR 24 HOURS)

IF UNFAMILIAR WITH MAINTENANCE PROCEEDURES, YOU SHOULD TAKE YOUR BOAT TO AN AUTHORIZED MARINE DEALER FOR SERVICE.

BOATING SAFETY INFO LINE 1-877-792-3926

WINTERIZATION AND STORAGE

When preparing to winterize your craft, be certain to read your owner's manual. If you are unsure of the appropriate winterization procedure for your type of boat, visit your local marine dealer for advice and service. The following is an overview of winterization and storage procedures:

STEP 1
Use an environmentally-friendly marine detergent or algae remover to clean the hull of your craft

STEP 2
Empty the bilge of any excess water and clean it using soap and water (or a marine-grade bilge cleaner)

STEP 3
Drain and flush the engine's cooling system

STEP 4
Fill the boat's fuel tank

STEP 5
Clean (or replace) the fuel filter

STEP 6
Remove the spark plugs and fog the engine cylinders with a rust inhibitor

STEP 7
Lubricate all moving parts

STEP 8
Clean off any excess grease, lubrication, dirt and marine life

TRANSPORTING YOUR BOAT

Transporting your boat safely isn't difficult—it's a matter of choosing the right towing equipment, using common sense when loading and unloading your boat and being confident with the techniques for driving safely with a trailer.

TIPS FOR DRIVING WITH A BOAT TRAILER

When driving, remember that your vehicle is longer and heavier than it was before the trailer was attached. To drive safely with a boat trailer in tow, you should:

- Accelerate slowly
- Turn using a wider radius to allow for the trailer
- Drive at a slower speed than normal
- Allow for greater braking distance
- Use extra caution if driving in high wind, heavy rain, fog or icy conditions

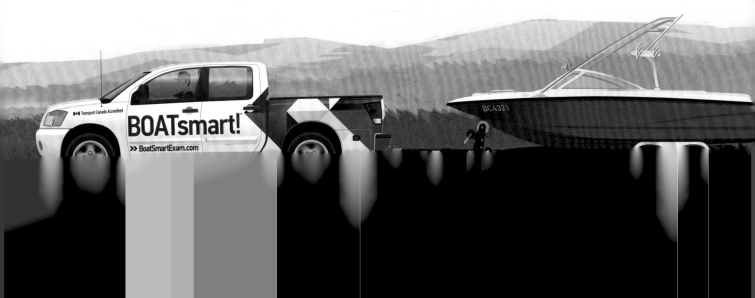

CHOOSING THE RIGHT TRAILER

To determine which style of trailer is right for you, consider the following:

- Is the width and length of the trailer suitable for the size of your boat?
- Is the weight capacity of the trailer suitable for the weight of your boat?
- Is the towing capacity of your vehicle suitable for the weight of your boat?
- Do all the operating lights work properly?
- Are the wheel bearings properly greased and able to operate smoothly?
- Does the coupler (located at the front end of the trailer) match the size of your vehicle's hitch ball?
- Is the trailer equipped with safety chains?
- Does your trailer require trailer brakes according to your local and provincial regulations?

SAFE BOATING TIP

Know the proper techniques for safe towing and practice driving and backing up with your trailer in a controlled environment before heading out on the road. Understand that you must comply with provincial and local laws with respect to trailer licensing, registration and operating lights.

Bunk-Style

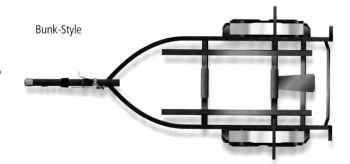

Roller-Style

TOWING YOUR BOAT

Attaching the trailer to your vehicle:

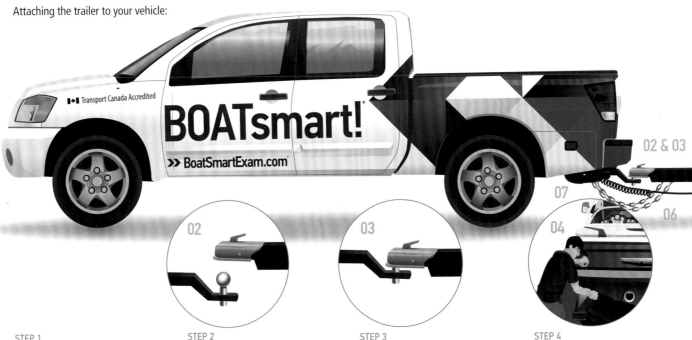

STEP 1

Before attaching the trailer to the vehicle, ensure that the trailer is properly balanced and level.

STEP 2

Position the vehicle or trailer so that the hitch ball is directly below the trailer's coupler and lower the trailer.

STEP 3

Securely fasten the tongue coupler and lock the trailer latch using a cotter pin or lock.

STEP 4

Using tie down straps, securely fasten the boat to the trailer.

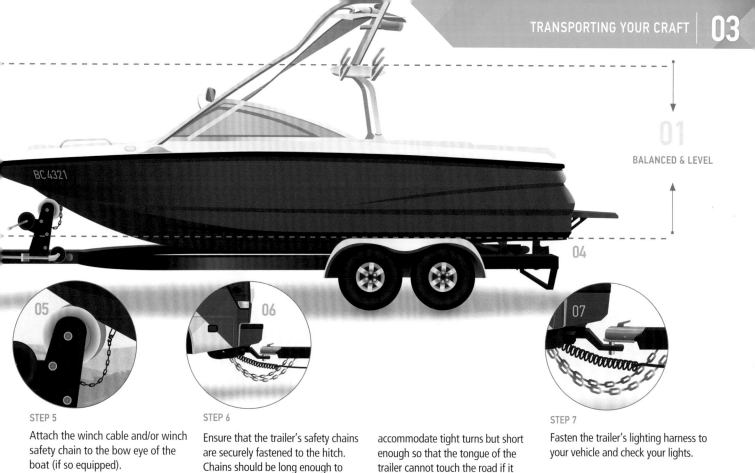

01

BALANCED & LEVEL

04

05

06

07

STEP 5

Attach the winch cable and/or winch safety chain to the bow eye of the boat (if so equipped).

STEP 6

Ensure that the trailer's safety chains are securely fastened to the hitch. Chains should be long enough to accommodate tight turns but short enough so that the tongue of the trailer cannot touch the road if it becomes dislodged from the hitch.

STEP 7

Fasten the trailer's lighting harness to your vehicle and check your lights.

HOW TO LAUNCH YOUR CRAFT

STEP 1

Make a visual check of the launch area: Is the ramp deep enough to launch your boat? Are there any overhead wires or obstructions?

UNLOCK INTERACTIVE CONTENT

Scan this page

Confident backing up with a trailer? Watch these tips!

STEP 2

Remove tie-down straps and unplug the trailer lights from your vehicle.

STEP 3

Ensure the bilge drain plug is properly installed.

STEP 4

Place all gear and safety equipment onboard the boat.

STEP 5

Ensure the winch is connected to the bow of the boat.

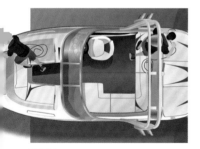

STEP 6

Attach a bow and stern line to the boat.

STEP 7

Slowly back the trailer into the water until the motor becomes submerged.

STEP 8

Test the operation of the motor by starting it and allowing it to warm up.

STEP 9

Shut down the motor and continue backing the trailer into the water until the boat begins to float.

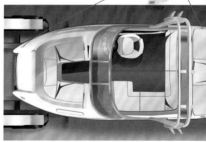

STEP 10

Use the bow and stern lines to guide the boat off the trailer and then remove the vehicle from the ramp.

HOW TO LOAD YOUR CRAFT

STEP 1

Secure the boat at the dock.

STEP 2

Back the trailer into the water until it is two-thirds submerged.

STEP 3

Turn off your vehicle and engage the emergency brake.

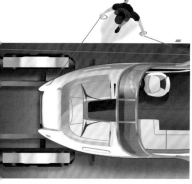

STEP 4

Position the boat on the trailer using the bow and stern lines—do not drive your boat onto the trailer.

STEP 5

Attach the winch line to the bow-eye of your boat. Pull the boat up onto the trailer using the winch.

STEP 6

Ensure the boat is properly seated and balanced on the bunks or rollers.

STEP 7

Once the boat is in position, lock the winch and attach the winch's safety chain (if so equipped).

STEP 8

Remove your vehicle and trailer from the ramp.

STEP 9

Once parked, attach the trailer lights and ensure they are working properly.

STEP 10

Remove the boat's bilge drain plug.

STEP 11

Secure the boat using tie-down straps (secure to the transom) before departing.

KNOWLEDGE OF LOCAL WATERWAYS

Safe boating is more than just a matter of operating your craft in a responsible manner. Before going out on the water, you should familiarize yourself with any local water hazards or dangerous conditions that may impede the safe operation of your craft. Failing to do so could increase the risk of injury or loss of life to you and your passengers.

You can refer to a Marine Chart or Nautical Publication to determine the location of waterway hazards for the area in which you will be operating. You can also talk to local operators and marinas that are familiar with the waters to gain valuable insight. Ask about specific hazards that you may encounter and any dangers that should be avoided. You should also determine the location of any ports of assistance in case of emergency.

Operators should check navigational references, such as marine charts, to determine the location of safe harbours or shelter that can serve as safe havens in the event of foul weather. Places of shelter can include marked areas for mooring as well as bays and dockage areas protected by breakwaters.

UNDERSTANDING LOCAL HAZARDS

Local water hazards can include:
- Low head dams
- Rapids
- Currents
- White water
- Tides
- Sudden winds
- Overhead cables
- Underwater cables
- Bridges
- Rapid build-up of high wave conditions

SAFE BOATING TIP
Rapids can be extremely dangerous:
- They have strong turbulent currents
- They conceal rocks just below the surface
- They can easily swamp a vessel and/or cause it to overturn
- They can overpower the vessel, causing loss of control
- They can easily cause personal injury or death to a person in the water

MARINE CHARTS AND NAUTICAL PUBLICATIONS

Marine charts are like a 'road map' of Canada's waterways. They indicate safe navigation routes and the location of markers, buoys and local hazards.

Marine publications and documents include 'Notices to Mariners', 'Sailing Directions' and 'Tide Tables'.

To navigate safely on Canada's waterways, every boater should know:
- How to use a compass along with marine charts
- How to plot a course using a marine chart
- Positioning methods
- How to locate and reference navigation aids on a marine chart
- How to properly use his/her electronic navigation equipment

Boat operators should check navigational references and publications (including tide tables) for water levels, times of low, slack and high tides and the direction of water flow. Marine charts and tide tables are published by the Canadian Hydrographic Services (CHS). More information can be obtained from the CHS at www.tides.gc.ca or 1-877-775-0790. If carrying nautical charts onboard they must be updated with information from Notices to Mariners available from CHS, to ensure they contain the latest changes to routes, buoys and water depth.

USING MARINE CHARTS AND NAUTICAL PUBLICATIONS

Marine charts depict:
- Depth
- Underwater hazards
- Location and character of charted shipping routes
- Aids to Navigation including lights, buoys and markers
- Traffic routes
- Adjacent coastal areas and landmarks around a body of water
- Navigational hazards
- Places to take shelter in the event of foul weather

The Charts and Nautical Publications Regulations require that operators carry the latest and largest scale versions of the following:
- Local Marine Charts
- The Required Publications and Documents (such as 'Current Atlases' and 'Tide Tables').

You may be exempt from these requirements if your vessel is under 100 tons and powered by oars or if you have substantial knowledge of the local waterway.

MANATEE BAY

TOPOGRAPHIC MAPS

Topographic maps can be useful to pleasure craft operators. Topographic maps depict natural and artificial features on land and include illustrations of shoreline contours, rocks, elevations and land features or hazards near or above the waterline.

In some instances, such as when a nautical chart or publication is unavailable for a body of water, topographic maps may aid in the navigation of local waterways. However, topographic maps are intended primarily for use on land by the general public. They do not depict underwater hazards, navigation aids, channels or anchorage areas. Topographic maps are published by Natural Resources Canada and other provincial authorities.

USING A COMPASS

You can use a magnetic compass to determine your direction and your position on a marine chart. However, be wary when using a compass—a magnetic compass can be affected **when in the proximity of metallic and electrical devices and may provide false information.**

Certain types of vessels engaged in a foreign voyage may require the use of a magnetic compass. Please refer to the Navigation Safety Regulations, Part 2-3 for specific requirements.

USING A MARINE GPS DEVICE

Marine GPS (Global Positioning System) devices can be used to identify your location. Some of today's systems are able to pinpoint your position to within several feet. Marine GPS devices are becoming a popular tool with boating enthusiasts.

Marine charts and nautical publications are now available in electronic format and can be used in conjunction with Marine GPS to offer boaters an extremely high degree of navigation certainty. Be sure to familiarize yourself with your Marine GPS and practice using it **before** heading out on the water. Marine GPS can provide your location, but you should always carry printed marine charts as a back-up in the event your Marine GPS fails.

Keep in mind that Marine GPS may only be accurate to within 30 m and automotive GPS will not provide the information you need on the water.

LOCAL FORECASTS

Understanding weather and water conditions is vital to boating safely. You should always check the local weather forecast to obtain current, relevant information **before heading out on the water.** Operating your vessel without prior knowledge of potential weather hazards may put your vessel and passengers at risk. Local forecasts are available from:

- Local newspaper
- Local radio
- Television weather forecast
- Radiotelephone
- The Meteorological Service of Canada
- www.weatheroffice.ec.gc.ca

VHF WEATHER FORECASTS

Environment Canada provides marine weather forecasts on the following frequencies:

ATLANTIC COAST AND GREAT LAKES

VHF Channel 21B, 25B and 83B

PACIFIC COAST

VHF Channel 21B and Wx1, 2, 3

Continuous weather broadcast information is available by telephone at (604) 666-3655 (Vancouver Region)

PERSONAL WEATHER OBSERVATIONS

In addition to checking the weather before you head out, you can use personal observations to monitor changing weather conditions:

- **Keep an eye to the sky:**
  Fog, dark clouds and lightning are obvious indications that bad weather is approaching
- **Barometric readings:**
  A rising barometer indicates fair weather, while a falling barometer indicates foul weather
- Pay particular attention to **shifts in wind direction and temperature** – both indicate that weather is changing

- **Be mindful of the West:**
  Foul weather usually approaches out of the West; however, storms from the East tend to be more powerful
- Be vigilant of **other boaters' movements** and monitor radio and weather channels frequently–ask for recommendations via radio if in unfamiliar waters

WIND

The Meteorological Service of Canada classifies all wind speed and weather warnings in Canada. The service has identified 5 categories of wind conditions that are defined in terms of their wind speed and the water conditions they create. Wind speed is measured in knots – **1 knot is equivalent to 1.85 km/h.**

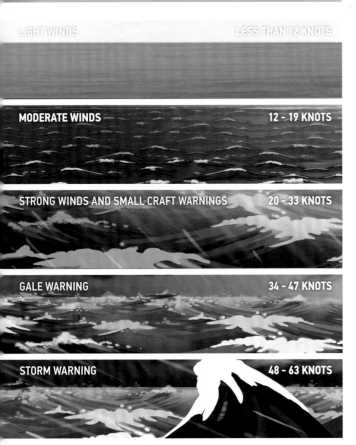

LIGHT WINDS — LESS THAN 12 KNOTS

MODERATE WINDS — 12 – 19 KNOTS

STRONG WINDS AND SMALL CRAFT WARNINGS — 20 – 33 KNOTS

GALE WARNING — 34 – 47 KNOTS

STORM WARNING — 48 – 63 KNOTS

LIGHT WINDS

Light winds have a wind speed of **less than 12 knots** (22 km/h) and water surface conditions that are calm or have waves up to 1.5 m in height. **Light wind conditions are suitable for most vessels and those operators with a moderate level of boating experience.**

MODERATE WINDS

Moderate winds have a wind speed of **12 to 19 knots** (22 to 35 km/h) and water surface conditions that are rough with waves from 1 to 3 m in height. **Inexperienced operators or vessels less than 6 m in length should not operate during such conditions.**

Operators of small vessels caught in a moderate winds advisory should attempt to cross waves at a 45° angle until sheltered waters are found. Ensure all passengers are wearing approved flotation devices.

STRONG WINDS AND SMALL CRAFT WARNINGS

Strong winds have sustained wind speeds in the range of **20 to 33 knots** (37 to 61 km/h). Water surface conditions during a strong winds advisory are **very rough** with waves 3 to 6 m in height. Environment Canada issues a **Small Craft Warning** when winds reach such levels. **It is not safe to operate a pleasure craft under these conditions.**

Operators of vessels caught in a strong winds advisory or small craft warning should take immediate action to ensure their safety. Turn on all navigation lights and attempt to cross waves at a 45° angle until sheltered waters are found. Reduce speed and proceed with caution, keeping a lookout for approaching boats and floating debris. If wind and wave conditions make it difficult to proceed, attempt to anchor your vessel until the storm subsides. Ensure all passengers are wearing approved flotation devices and keep passengers low in the boat and near the centerline.

GALE WARNING

Gale winds have a continuous speed of **34 to 47 knots** (63 to 87 km/h). Water surface conditions during a Gale Warning are **extremely rough** with waves 6 to 9 m in height. During such conditions, Environment Canada will issue a **Gale Warning. It is not safe to operate a pleasure craft under these conditions.**

Operators of vessels caught in a Gale Warning advisory should take immediate action to ensure their safety. Turn on all navigation lights and attempt to cross waves at a 45° angle until sheltered waters are found. Reduce speed and proceed with caution, keeping a lookout for approaching boats and floating debris. If wind and wave conditions make it difficult to proceed, attempt to anchor your vessel until the storm subsides.

Ensure all passengers are wearing approved flotation devices and keep passengers low in the boat and near the centerline. If your boat is taking on water, pump out bilges to keep the boat high in the water. Use an approved distress signal to signal your need for assistance if you are unable to make safe passage.

STORM WARNING

Storm winds have a continuous speed of **48 to 63** knots (89 to 117 km/h). Water surface conditions during a storm warning are **extremely rough** with waves over 8 m in height. During such conditions, Environment Canada will issue a **Storm Warning**. It is not safe to operate a pleasure craft under these conditions.

Operators of vessels caught in storm warning conditions should immediately signal distress and need of assistance.

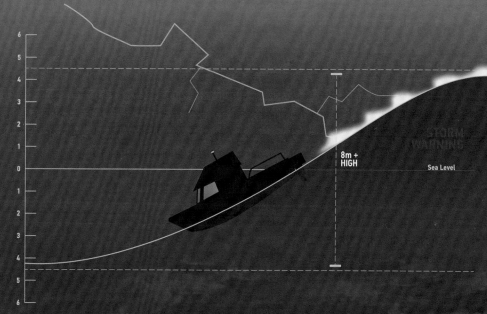

8m +
HIGH

Sea Level

STORM
WARNING

WHAT IS A TRIP PLAN?

A trip plan (also known as a float plan or sail plan) is a document that outlines your expected travel itinerary while on the water. A trip plan should be given to a responsible person on shore. In the event that you do not return from your trip on time, a trip plan can be used by search and rescue organizations to help pinpoint your whereabouts.

Download a trip plan at **BoatSmart**Exam.com®

PREPARING A TRIP PLAN

A trip plan should include:

- The name of your pleasure craft
- License number of your pleasure craft
- Type of craft (power or sail)
- Size and colour of your pleasure craft
- Type of engine
- Distinguishing features of the pleasure craft
- Your name, address and telephone number
- Number of persons onboard
- Trip description including:
  - Time of departure
  - Time of return
  - Proposed route
- Type of radiophone and channel monitored (if so equipped)
- List of safety equipment onboard including flares, life jackets, PFDs and life rafts
- Instructions in case of emergency

FILING A TRIP PLAN

WHERE TO FILE

A trip plan should be filed on shore with a responsible person, a marina, or with the local Canadian Coast Guard detachment. The person you file your trip plan with should know what to do in case of emergency.

CHANGING A TRIP PLAN

If you change plans during your trip you should notify the person with whom you've filed the plan. Doing so will inform the person of your correct whereabouts and avoid a false alarm or unnecessary emergency actions.

ON RETURN

Upon your return, you must remember to notify the person or organization with whom you filed the plan and inform them that you have returned safely. Failing to do so may result in a false alarm and the launch of a search and rescue operation.

TRIP PLAN BOATsmart! >>

BOAT INFORMATION:
BOAT NAME
REGISTRATION NUMBER
TYPE OF BOAT (POWER OR SAIL)
HULL COLOR(S)
TYPE OF ENGINE

HOME PORT
YEAR AND MAKE
BOAT SIZE (LENGTH)
DECK COLOR(S)
UNIQUE FEATURES

PASSENGER INFORMATION:
OPERATOR NAME
TELEPHONE NUMBER
PASSENGERS/CREW
1.
2.
3.

ADDRESS
NUMBER OF PASSENGERS/CREW
4.
5.
6.

TRIP DESCRIPTION:

SAFE BOATING TIP

Trip plans should always be left with a responsible person who knows what to do in case of emergency. Even for a short boating trip, you should let a responsible person know where you will be boating, when you are expected to arrive home and the distinguishing features of your boat.

Scan to download a BOATsmart!® Trip Plan

PLANNING AHEAD

Running out of fuel is the number one cause of boater distress. You should always be sure to plan your requirements and carry enough fuel.

As a general practice you should use the **rule of thirds** when considering the amount of fuel required:

- 1/3 out
- 1/3 back
- 1/3 in reserve

SAFETY PRECAUTIONS WHEN FUELING

Follow these common sense rules when fueling:

- Always use caution
- Do not overfill or spill fuel: spilling fuel into the engine or passenger compartment can increase the risk of explosion or fire
- Refuel during daylight hours when an artificial light source is not needed (the electrical current from the light source can ignite fuel vapours)
- Never smoke while refueling

REMEMBER:

Gasoline is highly explosive when mixed with air. Gas vapours will ignite when exposed to flame or spark, resulting in destruction of property, serious injury and death. Every boat that has a gasoline engine or uses propane devices, must have ignition-protected electrical devices.

This protection prevents sparks from escaping during use. You should only use electrical components that are clearly labelled as ignition protected and never modify or repair marine engines with automotive parts.

FUELING A BOAT

The following procedure is not only recommended for safety—it's the law.
When fueling a boat equipped with a gasoline or diesel engine, perform the following:

STEP 1

Ensure your boat is securely moored to the dock.

STEP 2

Shut down all motors.

STEP 3

Ask all passengers to disembark the craft and remain on shore.

STEP 4

Extinguish any open flames, including cigarettes and pilot lights.

STEP 5

Close all doors, windows, ports and any hatches.

STEP 6

Shut down all electrical equipment.

STEP 7

Have a fire extinguisher available in case of emergency.

STEP 8

Check for leaks and fuel odors.

STEP 9

When fueling at a pump, keep the gas nozzle against the rim of the filler pipe. This will ensure the pump is grounded and will reduce the risk of ignition due to static electricity.

STEP 10

Never overfill the fuel tank. Be sure to clean up any spillage and securely tighten the filler cap.

STEP 11

Open all doors, windows, hatches and portholes once refueling is complete.

STEP 12

If your boat is equipped with an enclosed engine compartment, you must operate the ventilation system (blower) for at least four minutes prior to engine start-up.

STEP 13

Re-check for the smell of fuel odors (do not re-start your engine if excessive fuel odors are detected).

STEP 14

Start the motor.

REFUELING A PORTABLE TANK

When refueling a portable container:

STEP 1

Ensure your boat is securely
moored to the dock.

STEP 2

Shut down all motors.

STEP 3

Extinguish any open flames, including cigarettes.

STEP 4

Disconnect the fuel line and move the tank
to the dock.

STEP 5

Always use a tank that has been
approved for use in Canada.

STEP 6

Check the fuel system (including the tank,
fuel line, and connectors) for any leaks.

STEP 7

For mixed gasoline: alternate the addition of gas
and oil as the tank is filled. Ensure gas and oil are
thoroughly mixed before reconnecting the fuel
system to the motor.

STEP 8

Once filled, place the tank back in the craft.
Reconnect the fuel line and re-check for leaks.

STEP 9

Start the motor.

FUELING A PWC

Some additional considerations should be taken when fueling a PWC:

STEP 1

Shut down the engine.

STEP 2

Ask all passengers to disembark the craft and remain on shore.

STEP 3

Extinguish any open flames, including cigarettes.

STEP 4

Visually check the gas separator for the presence of water–remove any traces of water before refueling.

STEP 5

Ensure the fuel selector switch is turned to the 'OFF' position.

STEP 6

For PWCs requiring mixed gasoline: always pre-mix gas and oil in an approved portable container before refueling the PWC.

STEP 7

For PWCs equipped with an oil injection system: ensure the oil tank is full with the approved oil for your craft.

STEP 8

Fill the tank.

STEP 9

Tighten the fuel filler cap and check for fuel odors.

STEP 10

Turn the fuel selector switch to the 'ON' position and restart the engine.

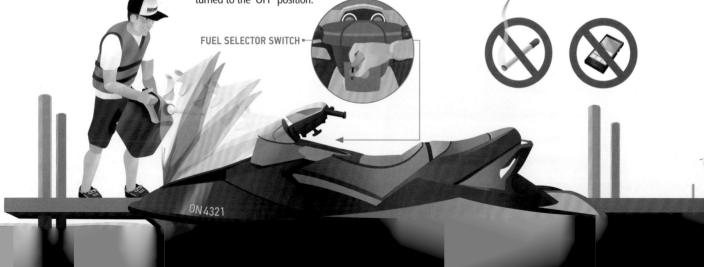

FUEL SELECTOR SWITCH

ON 4321

PRE-DEPARTURE CHECKLIST

Completing a Pre-Departure Checklist before getting underway is an excellent way to avoid unsuitable operating conditions and reduce the risk of a breakdown. You should always use a Pre-Departure Checklist to ensure that your boat has the right safety equipment onboard. It only takes a few minutes to fill out your checklist and it is time well spent!

Download a Pre-Departure Checklist at **BoatSmartExam.com**®

SAFE BOATING TIP

To prevent being in an emergency situation, operators are responsible for ensuring they have the boating experience and skill level for the planned trip BEFORE leaving the dock.

Scan to download
a BOATsmart!®
Pre-Departure Checklist

BOATsmart!

PRE-DEPARTURE CHECKLIST

FEDERALLY REQUIRED BOAT EQUIPMENT:
- [ ] PFD/LIFEJACKETS FOR EVERYONE ONBOARD (Coast Guard-approved)
- [ ] THROWABLE TYPE IV DEVICE (if boat is over 16 feet in length)
- [ ] FIRE EXTINGUISHER (fully charged)
- [ ] SOUND PRODUCING DEVICE

- [ ] VISUAL DISTRESS SIGNALS
- [ ] BACKFIRE FLAME CONTROL (if the boat has an inboard engine)
- [ ] NAVIGATION LIGHTS
- [ ] DOCUMENTATION (Boater Education Card, Registration documents)

ADDITIONAL RECOMMENDED EQUIPMENT:
- [ ] VHF-FM MARINE RADIO/ EPIRB/PLB
- [ ] CHARTS OF THE AREA
- [ ] FENDERS AND A BOAT HOOK
- [ ] MANUAL BILGE BUMP OR A BAILING DEVICE
- [ ] SPARE BATTERY
- [ ] PADDLES /OARS
- [ ] FLASHLIGHT AND BATTERIES
- [ ] FIRST-AID KIT
- [ ] MIRROR (to create a signal by reflecting sunlight off of it)
- [ ] EXTRA CLOTHING
- [ ] BINOCULARS

- [ ] ANCHOR AND LINE
- [ ] MAGNETIC COMPASS
- [ ] MOORING LINES AND A HEAVING LINE
- [ ] TOOL KIT AND SPARE PARTS (fuses, sparks, belts, etc)
- [ ] SPARE PROPELLER
- [ ] EXTRA FUEL AND OIL
- [ ] SEARCH LIGHT
- [ ] SUNSCREEN
- [ ] FOOD AND WATER
- [ ] CELL PHONE
- [ ] MARINE SANITATION DEVICE (if applicable)

PREPERATION:
- [ ] I HAVE ENOUGH FUEL FOR THE TRIP - 1/3 OUT, 1/3 BACK, 1/3 IN RESERVE
- [ ] I HAVE THOROUGHLY CHECKED THE CONDITION ON MY BOAT, IT'S ENGINE AND FITTINGS
- [ ] I HAVE COMPLETED A FLOAT PLAN AND FILED IT WITH A RESPONSIBLE INDIVIDUAL ON SHORE
- [ ] I HAVE REVIEWED EMERGENCY AND SAFETY PROCEDURES AND PRACTICED THE PROPER TECHNIQUES
- [ ] I HAVE REVIEWED EACH PASSENGER'S RESPONSIBILITIES BEFORE DEPARTING
- [ ] I HAVE EXPLAINED THE LOCATION AND CORRECT USE OF REQUIRED SAFETY EQUIPMENT WITH EACH PASSENGER

BOATING SAFETY INFO LINE 1-877-792-3926

INSTRUCTING YOUR PASSENGERS

As the boat operator, it is important to **talk to your passengers before leaving the dock**. Use your Pre-Departure Checklist as a discussion prompt to familiarize passengers with the following procedures:

- How to operate the craft in case of emergency
- The location of the craft's emergency kit
- How to rescue a person overboard
- How to properly use an approved life jacket or PFD

As the operator, you are responsible for instructing your passengers to:

- Always wear an approved life jacket or PFD
- Be aware that the effects of sunlight, motion, waves, wind and sound can impair their judgment
- Keep close to the centerline of the boat and as low as possible when moving around the boat
- Keep hands and feet inside the craft when departing or returning to the dock
- Refrain from consuming alcohol while onboard

Several boating safety organizations, including the Canadian Coast Guard Auxiliary, offer free courtesy checks for pleasure craft to help operators ensure they have the proper safety equipment onboard. These knowledgable boating experts can help to identify any potential problems.

MODULE 3 SUMMARY

Maintaining your equipment in proper working order will help you avoid emergency situations and reduce your operating costs. You should perform maintenance on your craft and equipment at the beginning of each season and at regular intervals throughout the season. The use of a maintenance checklist is recommended.

Understanding local water hazards and determining local weather conditions before you depart will help you avoid unsuitable operating conditions and potentially life threatening situations. Before heading out, you should consult marine charts for the waterway in which you plan to operate, and talk to local boaters and marine operators to gain valuable insight.

The Canadian Coast Guard recommends the use of a trip plan before heading out. A trip plan is used to identify your vessel and proposed route, and can be a significant aid to search and rescue organizations in an emergency. The use of a Pre-Departure Checklist is also highly recommended.

MODULE 3 QUIZ

1   THE CHARTS AND NAUTICAL PUBLICATIONS REGULATIONS REQUIRE WHICH OF THE FOLLOWING?

A   That boaters are required to carry marine charts under all circumstances
B   That boaters must carry the largest scale charts for the area in which they are navigating
C   That marine charts depict marina service locations
D   That if your boat is equipped with a marine GPS you are still required by law to have printed charts

2   WHAT SHOULD YOUR PASSENGERS DO WHEN YOU ARE REFUELING YOUR BOAT?

A   Stay onboard
B   Stay onboard but refrain from smoking
C   Disembark
D   Operate the 'blower'

3   WHAT IS THE PENALTY FOR A PERSON WHO KNOWINGLY OPERATES A BOAT IN UNSEAWORTHY CONDITION?

A   Charges will be laid under the Criminal Code
B   The suspension of the Captain's Certificate
C   The boat will be impounded for 60 days
D   Charges will be laid under the Collision Regulations

MODULE 3 QUIZ

4 UNDER WHAT CONDITIONS MIGHT A MAGNETIC COMPASS BE NEGATIVELY AFFECTED AND PROVIDE YOU WITH INCORRECT INFORMATION?

A   When the compass is on the inside of a boat cabin
B   When the compass is exposed to sunlight
C   When in the proximity of metallic and electrical devices
D   When held higher than 4 ft above the boat

5 MARINE CHARTS ARE PRIMARILY USED BY BOATERS FOR WHICH PURPOSE?

A   To aid in navigation and determine local hazards
B   To determine the position of waterway attractions
C   To mark the fastest route
D   To locate a marina

6 WHEN SHOULD YOU DETERMINE THE LOCAL WEATHER FORECAST??

A   Immediately after you head out
B   Before you head out
C   As long as its not storming, you don't need to worry
D   7 days prior to your departure

7 WHAT IS THE PURPOSE OF DE-ACTIVATING A TRIP PLAN (SAIL PLAN) UPON YOUR RETURN FROM A BOATING TRIP?

A   To alert commercial traffic that the waterway is now clear for use
B   To make sure search and rescue teams do not go looking for you
C   To meet the *Operation Regulation* requirement to de-activate a sail plan
D   To keep a map of the route in case the operator decides to repeat it

8 HOW LONG SHOULD YOU OPERATE THE ENGINE VENTILATION SYSTEM ('BLOWER') BEFORE STARTING THE ENGINE?

A   At least 2 minutes
B   At least 6 minutes
C   At least 4 minutes
D   It is not always necessary

9 WHAT IS THE BEST WAY TO ENSURE YOU HAVE ENOUGH FUEL ONBOARD?

A   Rule of thirds - 1/3 out, 1/3 back and 1/3 in reserve
B   Rule of halves - 1/2 out and back, 1/2 reserve
C   You should always fill your tank before departing
D   Calculate your gas mileage based on 5 nautical miles per gallon

10 WHICH LAW REQUIRES THAT YOU MAINTAIN YOUR BOAT AND EQUIPMENT IN SEAWORTHY CONDITION?

A   The *Boating Restriction Regulations*
B   The *Maintenance Regulations*
C   The *Criminal Code of Canada*
D   The *Contraventions Act*

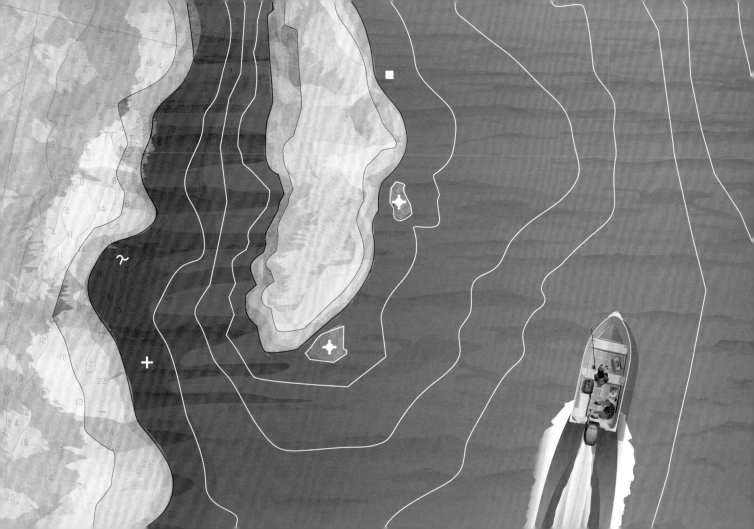

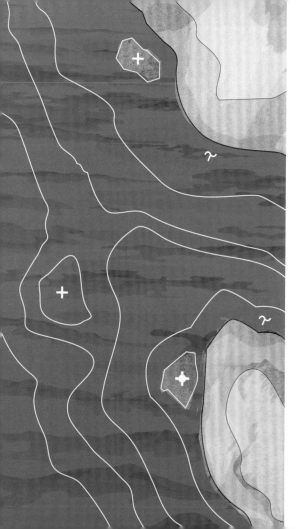

module 4
SAFE BOAT OPERATION

LOADING PEOPLE AND EQUIPMENT

Loading your boat improperly, either by overloading it or by uneven weight distribution, can result in unpredictable boat handling. This will increase your risk of being swamped by a wave and **may cause a capsizing emergency.**

When loading a pleasure craft:

STEP 1

Consult the pleasure craft's Compliance Notice and ensure that:
- Equipment and people do not exceed the 'recommended gross load capacity' of the craft.
- The number of people onboard does not exceed 'the equivalent number of adult persons' the craft is capable of safely carrying.

STEP 2

Ensure each passenger is wearing a properly-fitted and approved PFD or life jacket.

STEP 3

The operator should board first and then assist each passenger aboard.

STEP 4

Position equipment and people so that weight is equally distributed and as low as possible throughout the craft.

STEP 5

Each person should be properly seated and positioned before the next person comes aboard.

STEP 6

Ensure all equipment is securely fastened and stored properly to prevent uncontrolled shifting once the craft is underway—you should stow gear in lockers that are easily accessible in case of emergency and as low as possible to help stabilize the craft.

SAFE BOATING TIP

Always be sure to load people and equipment so that weight is equally distributed throughout your boat. This will keep your boat 'level' in the water, ensure greater stability and reduce the likelihood that your boat could capsize. Be sure to maintain the weight distribution of passengers and load while underway.

INSTRUCTIONS FOR PWC PASSENGERS

- Advise passengers as to the location of the PWC's safety equipment
- Passengers should read and understand the warning labels on the PWC
- Inform passengers that a PWC is less stable than a traditional vessel and that the PWC will become more unstable as each passenger boards the craft
- Passengers should keep their weight stable and evenly distributed
- Advise passengers to keep legs and arms within the craft at all times
- Remind passengers to keep away from the PWC's intake grate while the engine is running–items such as long hair, loose clothing, or PFD straps can become entangled in the moving parts of the jet intake system, resulting in severe injury or death
- Advise passengers that the jet propulsion system is powerful and water and/or debris exiting the jet thrust nozzle can cause severe injury–operators and passengers should avoid being close to the jet thrust nozzle at the rear of the machine
- Remind passengers to never place their feet or legs in the water to aid turning
- Passengers should hold onto the seat strap while underway

CASTING OFF

USE THE FOLLOWING PRECAUTIONS WHEN CASTING OFF:

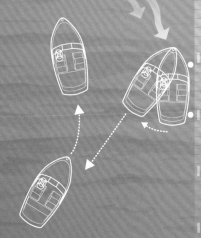

STEP 1

All passengers should be seated properly with their hands and feet inside the boat.

STEP 2

For boats equipped with enclosed engine compartments, operate the ventilation system (blower) for at least 4 minutes before starting the engine.

STEP 3

Start the engine:
- PWC operators should ensure the engine's kill switch (safety lanyard) is securely attached to their wrist or PFD at all times.

STEP 4

Check your surroundings and take into account any obstacles or other craft.

STEP 5

Untie all mooring lines and push the boat away from the dock:
- As you leave the dock, the stern of your boat will likely swing back towards the dock—push your boat well clear of the dock at both the bow and stern.
- Be careful if the wind is pushing your boat towards shore—you may need to operate in reverse, angling the stern away from the dock before pulling away, to avoid a potential collision with the dock.

STEP 6

Proceed slowly from the dock until it is safe to increase your speed.

STEP 7

Fast acceleration may cause passengers to lose their balance. Ensure all passengers are informed before any rapid acceleration occurs.

RETURNING TO THE DOCK (USING THE WIND OR CURRENT)

STEP 1 Ensure all passengers are seated securely with their feet and hands inside the craft.

STEP 2 Use the wind or current:

No wind or current:

- Turn your boat slowly as you approach the dock at a 45° angle in order to come to a parallel resting position–if necessary, use reverse to control the position of the boat.

Wind or current pushing the boat toward the dock:

- Approach the dock slowly at a 10° to 20° angle (you want the boat to drift towards the dock).

Wind or current pushing the boat away from the dock:

- Approach the dock at a manageable speed and at an angle steeper than 45°. The angle of approach is steeper when the wind or current is stronger.

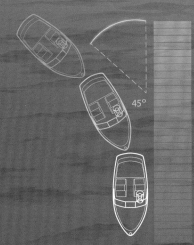

45°

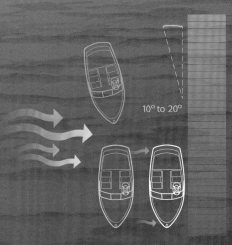

10° to 20°

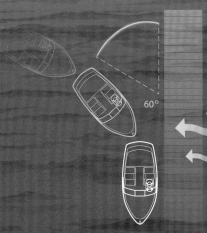

60°

STEP 3
Remember that your boat does not have brakes and will require a minimum distance to stop. The stopping distance will vary depending on speed, load, wind and water conditions.

MEMORY TIP:

There are 4 key factors to keep in mind when docking:

1) Preparation

2) Traffic

3) Wind

4) Current

Remember: the acronym for these words (P.T.W.C.) is exactly the same as this helpful and memorable sentence:

Position The Water Craft

DISEMBARKING YOUR CRAFT

WHEN DISEMBARKING:

STEP 1

Secure the craft.

STEP 2

Shut down the motor:
- PWC operators should remove the engine shut-off cord from the PWC to avoid accidental starting.

STEP 3

Securely fasten the craft to the dock.

STEP 4

Unload passengers one at a time.
- PWC operators should be aware that as each passenger exits the watercraft it may become unstable, and passengers should attempt to keep their weight distributed as they disembark from the PWC.

REMEMBER:

Never jump from the boat to the dock.

SAFETY UNDERWAY

Enjoying Canada's waterways is one of our greatest summer pastimes. While we all want to have fun and enjoy a day on the water, sharing the waterways with others means operating in a safe and courteous manner.

SAFETY UNDERWAY MEANS:

- Understanding and taking into account the **effects of being on the water**
- Choosing a **safe and appropriate speed**
- Knowing the proper techniques for **reducing risk** while operating at high speeds
- Knowing how to operate safely **amongst other boat traffic during the day or night** and sharing the waterways with others

EFFECTS OF BEING ON THE WATER

You should remember that certain **effects of being on the water can impair your judgment** and ability to operate your craft safely. These effects include

- The motion of your pleasure craft
- Sunlight
- Wind
- Waves
- Sound

These effects (individually or in combination with each other) may impair your balance, sense of coordination, reflexes, response time, eyesight, hearing and judgment. If you find that any of your senses are impaired you should immediately seek a safe harbour and shade yourself from direct sunlight.

Be aware of the effects of being on the water— both on yourself and on your passengers. Take steps to reduce these effects by ensuring that you wear appropriate protection from the elements including sunglasses, sunscreen and a visor or hat.

Be well rested when planning to operate your craft for extended periods and ensure that you consume ample liquids (such as water or juice) to keep hydrated. You should never consume alcohol or controlled substances when operating a pleasure craft.

HEAT EXHAUSTION

Heat exhaustion (or heat stroke) results from an abnormally elevated body temperature with accompanying physical and neurological symptoms. Heat exhaustion is a true medical emergency that can be fatal if not properly and promptly treated. Symptoms include nausea, vomiting, fatigue, weakness, headache, muscle cramps and dizziness.

Victims of heat exhaustion must receive immediate treatment to avoid permanent organ damage. First and foremost, cool the victim. Remove clothing, apply cool water to the skin and fan the victim to promote sweating and evaporation. Apply ice packs under armpits and groin and monitor body temperature and continue cooling efforts until body temperature cools to 38.3° C – 38.8° C.

CHOOSING A SAFE SPEED

The *Vessel Operation Restriction Regulations* impose standardized speed limits and shoreline speed zones (usually local in nature) and the *Collision Regulations* specify that it is an operator's responsibility to choose a safe speed.

Choosing a safe speed depends on:

- Your ability to see ahead–reduce your speed during fog, mist, rain and darkness
- Current, wind and water conditions
- How quickly your boat can change direction
- The boat traffic around you
- The presence of navigational hazards such as rocks and tree stumps
- Your distance from shore

Boaters should always abide by both posted and un-posted speed limits and be aware that various Canadian provinces have universal shoreline speed restrictions. These **un-posted restrictions require boaters to operate at 10 km/h or less when 30 m or closer to any shoreline.**

HIGH SPEED OPERATION

Pleasure craft operating at high speeds require a greater stopping distance. Operators driving their boats at high speeds should ensure they are able to **react effectively** in emergency situations, including sudden changes in water, weather and visibility conditions.

Be aware that high-speed operation reduces the amount of time you have to react in an emergency. You should always use caution and be more attentive when operating at high speeds.

REMEMBER:
Always operate at a speed that **allows you to take effective action** to avoid collisions.

TRIM

Your boat's trim is the angle of the boat in the water. Too much weight towards the bow of the boat will cause the front of the boat to plow down into the water. Too much weight towards the stern of the boat will cause the boat to bounce on the water. Either condition can result in poor and uncontrollable handling.

When properly 'trimmed', the gunwales of the craft should be parallel to the water. Trim can be controlled by altering the position of equipment and people in the craft. For craft equipped with power trim, the operator can adjust the trim of the boat by changing the angle of the motor/outdrive or 'trim tabs' that are affixed to the transom.

ACCELERATING AND PLANING

When accelerating, your boat will tend to leave the water and hydroplane onto the surface. Initially, this will lift the bow of the boat by several degrees and diminish your ability to see over the bow of your craft. To correct this situation, simply accelerate slightly to achieve full plane and your boat will regain a horizontal trim position.

CONTROLLING A PLEASURE CRAFT

STEERING

You should look in all directions (including behind to the stern) before turning your craft. Take note of the position of other boats and their relative speed. Once a safe direction has been established, **turn your boat in a predictable manner.** You should avoid rapid and unexpected manoeuvers as other boaters will not be able to predict your movements.

Most pleasure craft steer as water passes over the rudder or outdrive and is forced astern by the propeller. If power to the propeller is cut, the operator can still steer the craft as long as the boat is still moving (coasting) through the water.

STOPPING

To stop your craft, pull back on the throttle using a smooth, even motion. Your craft will slow to idle speed. To stop your craft completely, move the throttle lever to the neutral position. Always allow for enough distance for your boat to coast to a complete stop.

ON4321

TRIM

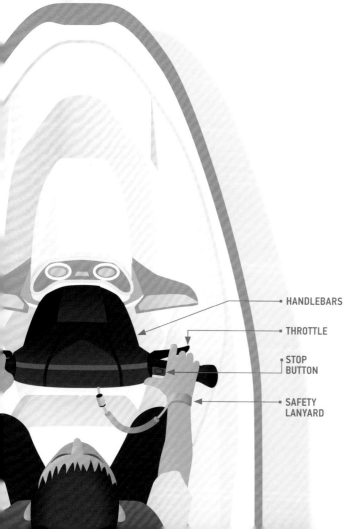

HANDLEBARS

THROTTLE

STOP
BUTTON

SAFETY
LANYARD

STEERING A PWC

Personal watercraft steer as high-pressure water passes through the craft's jet-propulsion system. Water is forced through the steering nozzle at the stern of the PWC. The steering nozzle is controlled by the handlebars, which the operator can turn left or right.

REMEMBER:
As a PWC's throttle lever is released to idle position, less water is forced through the system, and therefore less steering or directional control is available. If the engine is shut off, all directional control is lost. **You need to apply throttle in order to steer a PWC.**

STOPPING A PWC

You can stop a PWC by releasing the throttle lever, pressing the stop button or disconnecting the safety lanyard. PWCs coast farther and require more distance to stop than traditional pleasure craft. PWC operators should remember that a **minimum of 75 m** is required to stop from full throttle—exact stopping distance depends on the type and size of PWC being operated and the prevailing water and wind conditions.

Never use the PWCs reverse (if so equipped) to stop. You or your passenger(s) could be unexpectedly ejected towards the handlebars or thrown from the craft.

REMEMBER:
Become familiar with the stopping operations of your PWC by practicing in a safe, controlled area. Always leave ample distance between yourself and other craft.

HANDLING ROUGH WATER CONDITIONS

When boating in rough water you should adjust your boat's speed as appropriate to the water conditions. Slow down and use caution. Adjust your speed so that the bow of your craft does not become buried in a wave. You should never attempt to jump waves.

If you find yourself in increasingly high seas, you should make your way to a sheltered mooring, such as a protected bay, cove, or breakwater. If wave and water conditions make it unsuitable to operate safely, immediately set anchor and signal your need for help.

CROSSING A WAKE

When attempting to cross a wake, you should reduce your speed and alter your course to cross the wake at a 45° angle. Be aware of traffic that may be in your path as you cross to the other side of the wake. Once you have crossed the wake, resume your speed and course.

PWC operators should cross the wake at a 90° angle. Doing so will help maintain lateral stability. You should never attempt to jump a wake.

45°

OPERATING IN BAD WEATHER

Operating in bad weather is primarily a matter of avoiding collisions. Use the following techniques to avoid collisions in bad weather:

PROCEED WITH CAUTION

- Be able to stop in a short distance rather than having to resort to unexpected evasive manoeuvers

PLACE LOOKOUTS

- If you have passengers onboard, place them near the bow and stern as effective lookouts—operate with caution during high wave conditions when other craft may not be visible

LOOK AND LISTEN

- You and your passengers should 'look out' for other craft and navigational aids by both sight and hearing

NAVIGATION LIGHTS

- Use your craft's navigation lights during periods of restricted visibility to alert other boaters to your position

STOP YOUR ENGINES

- If you are underway in heavy fog, stop your engines at specific intervals to listen for fog signals from other vessels or marker buoys

USE YOUR RADAR

- Radar is your best option when visibility conditions are reduced—if you have a passive radar reflector it should be displayed during periods of restricted visibility

ON4321

Anchors have several uses:

- In the event of a breakdown   • During severe weather conditions
- An anchor is also useful in non-emergency situations (such as when swimming from the stern or securing for an overnight stay)

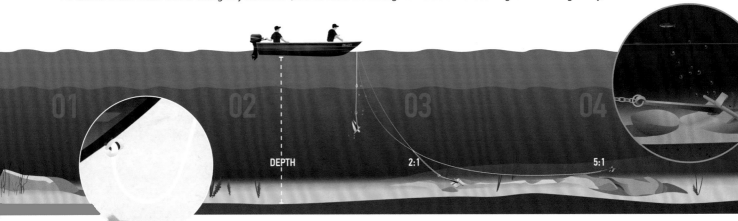

DEPTH   2:1   5:1

STEP 1

Ensure the **inboard end** of the anchor line is securely attached **to the pleasure craft**. Ensure the **outboard end** of the anchor line is securely fastened **to the anchor**.

STEP 2

Slowly lower the anchor over the bow or side of the craft until it reaches bottom. **Note the distance to the bottom** or note the length of rope used for the anchor to reach bottom. Never throw the anchor over the side of the boat.

STEP 3

Let the boat drift rearward or operate the engine astern (in reverse). **Let out an additional 5-10 times more anchor line than the depth of the water** and securely fasten the desired length to the boat.

STEP 4

At only 2x and 4x depth, the anchor can dig in but there is too much upward pull on the anchor line (rode). At a length of 5 to 10 times the water's depth, the rope lies flat on the bottom and pulls the anchor in deeper.

UNLOCK INTERACTIVE CONTENT

Scan this page

Pick the right anchor for your boat.

CHOOSING LANDMARKS

Once the anchor is set, choose two fixed landmarks on the horizon and occasionally check your relative position to ensure that you are not drifting.

SWING

Never secure the anchor to the stern of the craft.

If the wind changes direction, your boat will swing with the stern into the wind. Smaller boats can be easily swamped by waves crashing over the transom.

RIGHT OF SWING

If you are preparing to set anchor in an anchorage among other boats, remember that the first craft into anchorage has the **'right of swing'**. Other boats may 'swing' with changes in wind direction. Always allow for another craft's right of swing and anchor well clear.

RETRIEVING THE ANCHOR

To retrieve the anchor, slowly pull on the anchor line, move the boat forward until the anchor frees itself from the bottom, bring the anchor onto the craft and fasten securely.

SHARING THE WATERWAYS

Over 10 million boaters enjoy Canada's waterways each year. All boaters should be knowledgeable of and abide by the *Collision Regulations* and use common sense and courtesy while underway.

You should never create a hazard or stress to yourself, to your fellow operators or to the local habitat:

- Never operate close to swimmers and the personal property of others
- Ensure that your wake and wash will not cause personal injury, erosion of the shoreline or damage to personal property
- Use common sense and courtesy when operating close to non-powered craft
- Reduce your vessel's wake when passing small non-powered boats such as canoes, kayaks and rowboats as they can be easily swamped and capsized by your wake

OPERATING NEAR SWIMMERS

Operating a motorized boat near swimmers is extremely dangerous and against the law. Always keep well away from designated swimming areas.

Swimming areas in Canada are designated by swimming buoys that are white in colour. However, not all swimming areas may be marked. When operating near shore, keep a lookout for swimmers, including those persons engaged in underwater activities such as snorkeling or diving.

SAFE BOATING TIP
Remember: the sun's glare can make it difficult to spot swimmers in the water.

STAYING CLEAR OF DIVERS

Vessels and persons engaged in diving activities are required to display flags indicating their activities.

The boat from which divers are diving may display the **blue and white Code Flag 'A'** which indicates, 'I have a diver down: keep well clear at slow speed.' The *Collision Regulations* Rules 18 and 27 require that all operators take early and substantial action to steer well clear of any vessel that displays a Code Flag 'A'.

A **red and white diving flag (carried on the top of a white buoy)** marks an area where diving is in progress. Always be sure to keep a lookout for and steer clear of diving flags.

SAFE BOATING TIP

The red and white diving flag marks the general area where diving is in progress. **Keep in mind that it is easy for divers to stray from the area marked by a diving buoy.** Always exercise extreme care, slow down and avoid boating in waters frequented by divers.

CODE FLAG "A"   RED AND WHITE DIVING FLAG

WAKE AND WASH

Operators are responsible for the wake and wash of their craft:

- **WAKE** is caused by the boat moving through the water and **displacing** it
- **WASH** is the disrupted water following from the stern of the boat and is caused by the motion of the propeller

A number of provinces have adopted a province-wide speed limit of 10 km/h within 30 metres of shore. Although not posted, these speed limits are in effect on inland waterways. Some exceptions apply, such as when towing a water-skier or operating in rivers less than 100 m wide. As of the date of printing, these speed limits apply in Alberta, Manitoba, Saskatchewan, Ontario and British Columbia. Boaters should check with their provincial authorities for more information.

WAKE

WASH

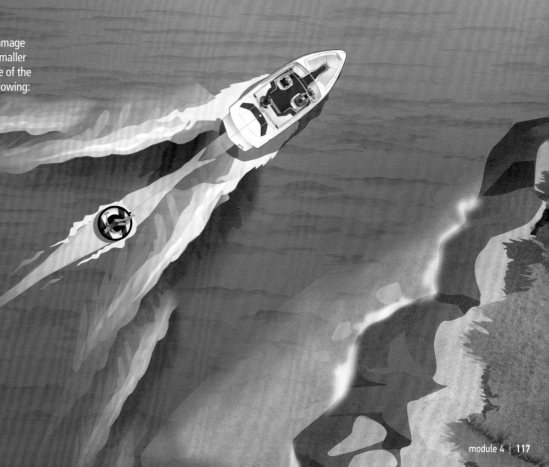

REDUCING THE EFFECTS OF WAKE AND WASH

Your craft's wake and wash can cause damage to the shoreline and can be a danger to smaller craft. When operating your craft be aware of the effects of your wake and wash on the following:

- Swimmers and bathing areas
- Docks
- Wildlife
- Shoreline erosion
- Smaller craft (such as fishing boats)
- Non-powered craft (such as canoes)
- Water-skiers
- Divers
- Areas of anchorage
- Other anchored or grounded vessels

If operating in or near such areas you should adjust the speed of your craft to reduce the effects of wake and wash. Doing so will ensure that you avoid the risk of personal injury, shoreline erosion and damage to personal property.

ENVIRONMENTAL RESPONSIBILITY

It is illegal to pollute Canadian waterways. Always use caution when refueling and be sure not to spill excess fuel into the water. When operating your craft, be mindful of and respect natural inhabitants and ecosystems. Nesting areas and spawning grounds need to be protected in order for ecosystems to function properly. Always keep well away from undeveloped shoreline areas.

You are prohibited from dumping oil, litter or waste overboard. Even small oil spills may cause serious long-term effects. Waste from marine toilets must be held in a holding tank and pumped out at an approved marine facility. Boaters are also prohibited from dumping bilge water containing oil or other chemicals overboard. You should check your bilge on a regular basis to ensure it's free of oil, grease and chemicals. If chemical pollutants are found in the bilge, use an environmentally-friendly absorbent product to soak up chemical waste. You must report to government authorities any discharge of a pollutant from your vessel that occurs, or the probability that such discharge will occur where the discharge is prohibited by the *Canada Shipping Act 2001*.

INVADING SPECIES

In recent years, Canada's waters have been under threat from aquatic plants, fish and invertebrates (mussels, snails etc.) that originate from other parts of the world, and that have been introduced (accidentally or intentionally) to Canada's waterways. With no natural predators, high reproductive rates and superior survival capabilities, these 'invading species' can rapidly take over Canada's waterways and wetlands with harmful effects on our native fish, wildlife, habitats and ecosystems. Invading species include Eurasian Watermilfoil, Purple Loosestrife and Zebra Mussels.

Invading species are spread by recreational boats and watercraft, as well as fishing equipment. Before entering any body of water you should clean your boat to remove foreign species and reduce the likelihood of spreading invading species. Inspect your boat, trailer and equipment. Remove visible plants or animals. Drain water from your boat's motor, live wells and bilge or transom wells on land and away from any waterway.

Wash and dry your boat, trailer and equipment. Remember that some species can survive out of water. Use one (or all) of the following methods to clean your boat of invading species:

- Rinse with hot tap water (at least 40° C)
- Spray with high pressure water (250 psi)
- Dry your boat and equipment before moving to another body of water

Anglers should keep empty bait buckets on land and away from the shoreline. They should consult provincial fishing regulations for information about the use of baitfish.

Never release live bait from one body of water to another. Report sightings or obtain information from your local provincial resource agency.

BLACK WATER

Raw, untreated sewage is called 'black water'. All boats fitted with a marine toilet must be equipped with a holding tank where black water can be stored until it can be disposed of at an approved pump-out station.

Allowing black water to escape into Canada's waterways is against the law. Serious bacterial infections can occur amongst swimmers, and black water has a negative effect on our environment. Dual systems with 'Y' valves (which allow waste to be dispelled from the boat) are illegal and must be retrofitted. Portable toilets are legal only if they are securely fastened to the craft and have a permanent fixture enabling them to be emptied at an approved facility. If you're planning an extended trip, you should plan to use onshore facilities wherever possible.

NOISE POLLUTION

Pleasure craft are not permitted within 5 nautical miles (9.26 km) of any Canadian shore unless they are fitted with a noise muffling device. A 'wet exhaust', where noise is muffled by cooling water discharged through the exhaust pipe, is not considered a noise muffling device. Operators should check with their local Canadian Coast Guard for any exemptions to this rule.

Boaters should remember that sound travels further on water than on land. Operating continuously in one area disturbs both those on land and on water. Don't 'buzz' around in one area, keep loud music to a minimum and respect those on shore, as well as your fellow boaters.

TOWING

Towing a water-skier, wakeboarder, kneeboarder or other towable device requires the use of a spotter. A spotter is a person who observes the person being towed at all times. The spotter notifies the driver if there is a need for a change in speed and/or direction as indicated by the skier's hand signals. The spotter can also notify the driver in case of emergency.

The driver should never watch the skier. The driver should always concentrate on driving the boat in a safe manner, keeping well clear of other boats, skiers, swimmers and hazards.

SAFE BOATING TIP
When 'dropping off' a water-skier at the dock, do not run parallel to the shore in shallow water. Keep your distance and let the person swing into shore. This will ensure the person being towed does not hit bottom or any underwater hazards.

RULES AND REGULATIONS

Obey the following rules when towing a water-skier—it's the law:

- A spotter must be in the boat at all times
- The towing vessel must be equipped with an extra seat for each person that is being towed in case an emergency recovery is necessary
- Only personal watercraft designed to carry 3 or more people can be used for towing a water-skier
- The person being towed must wear an approved flotation device (a 'ski belt' is not considered to be an approved flotation device)
- The towing vessel **cannot be operated by remote control**
- Do not tow water-skiers from one hour after sunset to sunrise
- It is a criminal offence, as governed by the *Criminal Code of Canada*, to tow a person after dark

HAND SIGNALS

Both the spotter and the person being towed must understand and be able to communicate using standardized hand signals.

SPEED OK

TURN LEFT

TURN RIGHT

OK

RETRIEVAL

STOP

SLOWER

FASTER

BACK TO DOCK

ON4321

MODULE 4 SUMMARY

Operating in a safe and responsible manner is every boater's obligation. Be sure that you understand how to properly control your craft and are aware of its unique handling characteristics.

After studying this module you should understand the proper procedures for casting off and returning to the dock. You should also be aware of the effects of being on the water and know how to adjust for them. Remember to minimize the effects of your wake and wash when operating close to shore and near non-powered craft.

Knowing how to anchor your craft correctly is useful when stopping for an overnight stay or when swimming from the stern of your craft. It's also a valuable technique that can be used in an emergency situation, such as during a storm or if a mechanical breakdown occurs.

Be sure that you understand the rules and regulations for towing a tube, water-skiers or wakeboarders. Always use a spotter and operate with caution when towing your passengers.

MODULE 4 QUIZ

1   YOU SHOULD ALWAYS ENSURE WHICH OF THE FOLLOWING WHEN ANCHORING YOUR CRAFT?

A   Ensure the inboard end of the anchor line is securely attached to the anchor
B   Ensure the outboard end of the anchor line is securely attached to the craft
C   Ensure the inboard end of the anchor line is securely attached to the craft
D   Ensure the anchor line is 10 times the length of your craft

2   WHEN IS A SAFE TIME TO OPERATE YOUR BOAT CLOSE TO A DESIGNATED SWIMMING AREA?

A   After sunset on waterways with low traffic
B   You should never operate close to a designated swimming area
C   Before sunrise on waterways with low traffic
D   When there are no swimmers visible

3   WHEN MUST A SPOTTER BE PRESENT WHEN TOWING A PERSON WATER-SKIING, WAKEBOARDING OR USING ANY OTHER TOWABLE DEVICE?

A   A spotter must always be present
B   Only when using a PWC
C   Only when towing multiple people
D   Only when towing someone at night

MODULE 4 QUIZ

4   WHEN LOADING PASSENGERS ONTO YOUR CRAFT, WHERE SHOULD YOU BEST POSITION THEM?

A   Near the bow of the craft
B   So that weight is equally distributed throughout the craft
C   Near the stern of the craft
D   Doesn't matter

5   WHICH OF THE FOLLOWING IS NOT ENVIRONMENTALLY-FRIENDLY AND SHOULD NOT BE DISCHARGED FROM YOUR BOAT?

A   Green water
B   Clear water
C   Black water
D   There are no restrictions on discharging water

6   WHAT DOES THE BLUE AND WHITE INTERNATIONAL CODE FLAG 'A' INDICATE?

A   'I have broken down: please get help'
B   'I am engaged in fishing activities: keep well clear at slow speed'
C   'I have a diver down: keep well clear at slow speed'
D   It is used to identify search and rescue vessels

7   THE WATER DISPLACED BY THE MOVEMENT OF A BOAT IS CALLED?

A   Wake
B   Wash
C   Tide
D   Surf

8   ARE PLEASURE CRAFT LEGALLY REQUIRED TO BE FITTED WITH A NOISE MUFFLING DEVICE (SUCH AS A MUFFLER)?

A   Pleasure craft are not required to be fitted with a noise muffling device
B   A noise muffling device is only required when using your boat within 9.26 km (5 nautical miles) of a Provincial Park
C   Only boats larger than 20 m are required to have a noise muffling device
D   Pleasure craft are not permitted within 9.26 km (5 nautical miles) of any shore unless they are fitted with a noise muffling device

9   WHY SHOULD YOU CONSIDER 'RIGHT OF SWING' WHEN ANCHORING YOUR CRAFT?

A   Considering 'right of swing' will ensure you do not anchor in a navigational channel
B   Considering 'right of swing' will ensure you do not anchor in a shipping lane
C   Considering 'right of swing' will ensure you leave enough room between you and other anchored craft
D   'Right of swing' ensures you display the proper anchor lights

10   SOME BOATS AND PWCS CAN TRAVEL AT VERY HIGH SPEEDS. WHAT SHOULD YOU CONSIDER WHEN OPERATING AT HIGH SPEEDS?

A   You have the right-of-way if traveling faster than other boats
B   You do not have as much time to react or stop in an emergency
C   You can steer quickly in an emergency
D   You can stop quickly in an emergency

module 5
NAVIGATION & RIGHT-OF-WAY RULES

THE COLLISION REGULATIONS

The *Collision Regulations* **govern the rules that prevent collisions on the high seas and inland waterways.** These rules apply to all vessels and to all waters in Canada. As such, the *Collision Regulations* govern the following:

- Navigation
- Right-of-way rules
- Lookout rules

YOUR RESPONSIBILITIES

As a Canadian boater, you must use all available means, appropriate to the prevailing circumstances and conditions, to make a full appraisal of navigation situations and determine if the risk of collision exists. This means that **you must know, understand and abide by Canada's navigation rules at all times.** You must also use good judgement and remain alert in case the operators of other boats are not abiding by the navigation rules. **Don't presume the actions of others and always proceed with caution.**

DETERMINING RIGHT-OF-WAY

First, you should become familiar with **right-of-way terminology**:

STAND-ON CRAFT

Boats **with the right-of-way** are called '**stand-on craft**'. Stand-on craft are able to maintain speed and direction when approaching other vessels.

GIVE-WAY CRAFT

Boats that **do not have the right-of-way** are called '**give-way craft**'. Give-way craft must take early and substantial action to steer clear of stand-on craft, altering speed and direction to avoid a collision.

SEVERAL FACTORS DETERMINE WHICH CRAFT HAS THE RIGHT-OF-WAY:

1 The **type of craft you're operating**
2 The **type(s) of craft you're approaching**
3 The **position and direction from which other craft are approaching**
4 The **type of waterway** on which you're operating

SAFE BOATING TIP

The *Collision Regulations*, Rule 5, requires all pleasure craft operators to maintain a proper lookout by both sight and hearing at all times.

TYPE OF CRAFT

The types of craft approaching each other determine which operator has the right of way:

- **Emergency craft** always have the right-of-way and all pleasure craft operators should steer clear and yield to emergency craft

- **Never pass between a tug and its tow** (as it may be using a submerged towline)

- **Keep clear of docked ferries**, ferries in transit and cable ferries which operate with a submerged tow cable from the bow and stern (listen for large ship horns blasting one prolonged blast, which indicates departing a dock)

- Both powerboats and sailboats must take early and substantial action to keep well clear of **vessels engaged in fishing activities** (those vessels operating with fishing nets and trawls)

- Power-driven vessels must keep out of the way of any vessel that is **not under command**

- **Non-powered craft** including sailboats, canoes, paddleboats, sailboards and racing shells generally have the right-of-way over power-driven pleasure craft

- All motorized boats and sailboats under 20 m in length must steer clear of **larger, less manoeuverable vessels**

- **'Sport' fishing boats** and waterski boats are considered manoeuverable craft and operators of these craft must follow the same rules as all pleasure boats

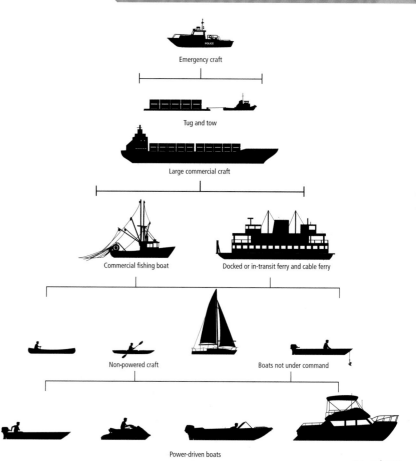

Emergency craft

Tug and tow

Large commercial craft

Commercial fishing boat

Docked or in-transit ferry and cable ferry

Non-powered craft

Boats not under command

Power-driven boats

APPROACHING NON-POWERED CRAFT

When approaching a non-powered craft, such as a sailboat or canoe, you are the **give-way craft** and do not have the right-of-way.

You must take early and substantial action to keep well clear of non-powered craft. You should alter your speed and course, and approach non-powered craft with caution.

APPROACHING POWER-DRIVEN CRAFT

POSITION AND DIRECTION

Power-driven vessels approaching each other establish right-of-way by determining each boat's position relative to the other. To properly understand right-of-way, you must be able to recognize the 'sectors' of navigation, including the port sector, starboard sector and stern sector. You should reference these sectors relative to other boat traffic in order to determine who has the right-of-way.

OPERATING RULES – KEEPING IT SIMPLE

PORT

If a power-driven boat approaches your boat from the port sector, maintain your course and speed with caution **You are the stand-on craft.**

STARBOARD

If any vessel approaches your boat from the starboard sector, you must keep out of its way. **You are the give-way craft.**

PORT   STARBOARD

112.5°   112.5°

135°

STERN

STERN

If any vessel approaches your boat from the stern (from behind your boat) you should maintain your course and speed with caution. **You are the stand-on craft.**

THE DANGER ZONE - GIVE WAY ZONE

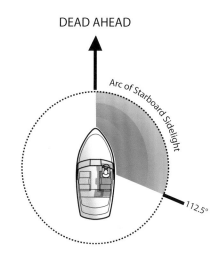

DEAD AHEAD

Arc of Starboard Sidelight

112.5°

Your starboard sector (the sector defined by your green starboard sidelight) is the 'Danger' or Give-Way Zone. When another boater sees your green light, he or she has the right-of-way. In this situation you will see the port side of the other boat and its red port sidelight. You must take early and substantial action to avoid a collision.

HEAD-ON APPROACH 01

When power-driven boats approach each other head-on, neither boat has the right-of-way.

Both operators (A and B) must take early and substantial action to steer clear of each other and steer to starboard (to the right) as soon as possible in order to avoid a collision.

PORT (LEFT) APPROACH 02

If a power-driven boat (B) is approaching from your port (left) sector you are the **stand-on craft** (A) and have the right-of-way. You should **maintain** your speed and course and be ready to take evasive action.

The approaching boat (B) must take early and substantial action to avoid your boat by reducing its speed and changing direction.

01

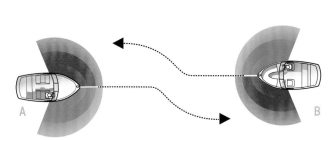

02

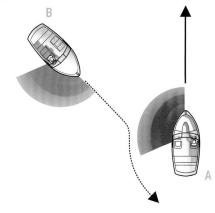

STARBOARD (RIGHT) APPROACH 03

If a power-driven boat (B) is approaching from your starboard (right) sector you are the **give-way craft** and do not have the right-of-way.

You must take early and substantial action to **keep well clear** of the other boat by altering your speed and course.

OVERTAKING 04

If you are overtaking another power-driven boat (B) from the stern (from behind) you are the **give-way craft** (A) and do not have the right-of-way.

You must take early and substantial action to **keep well clear of the other boat** by altering your speed and course. You should pass at a safe distance to the port (left) or starboard (right) side of the other boat. However, if a safe route exists, you should always attempt to pass the boat on the starboard side.

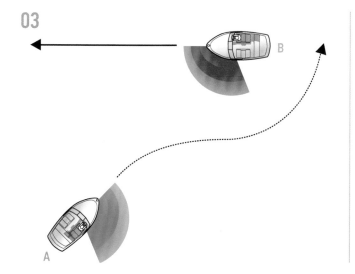

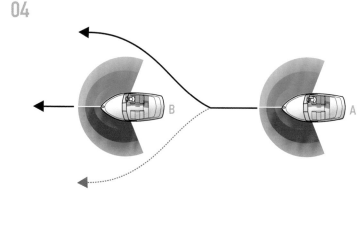

PORT (LEFT) APPROACH
YOU ARE: **STAND-ON CRAFT**

STARBOARD (RIGHT) APPROACH
YOU ARE: **GIVE-WAY CRAFT**

HEAD-ON APPROACH
NEITHER BOAT HAS THE RIGHT-OF-WAY

OVERTAKING
YOU ARE: **GIVE-WAY CRAFT**

USING SOUND SIGNALS FOR NAVIGATION

1 SHORT BLAST INDICATES:
I am altering my course to starboard (to the right)

2 SHORT BLASTS INDICATE:
I am altering my course to port (to the left)

3 SHORT BLASTS INDICATE:
I am operating my boat in reverse

5 RAPID BLASTS INDICATE:
I am unsure of the other boat's intentions

1 LONG BLAST INDICATES:
I am leaving the dock and am a motorized boat of 12 m or longer

EXCEPTION:
If you're operating a boat on the Great Lakes:

- 1 short blast indicates that I want to pass you on my boat's port (left) side
- 2 short blasts indicate that I want to pass you on my boat's starboard (right) side

DURING PERIODS OF REDUCED VISIBILITY:

- Sailboats should sound 1 long blast followed by 2 short blasts
- Motorized boats should sound 1 long blast every 2 minutes
- Boats at anchor should blast a sound signal rapidly for about 5 seconds every minute

SAFE OPERATION IN RESTRICTED VISIBILITY

Boaters should take additional care when operating at night or during periods of restricted visibility such as fog, darkness or heavy rain.

REMEMBER:

If you are operating a pleasure craft and you are not in sight of other vessels due to poor visibility, you are required to proceed at a safe speed that is appropriate for the prevailing circumstances and visibility conditions (as described in the *Collision Regulations* Rule 19).

NAVIGATING AT NIGHT

Right-of-way and navigation rules are the same whether operating during the day or at night. However, **while operating at night or during periods of restricted visibility you must determine the speed, position, and size of other boats according to the navigation lights they exhibit.**

Navigation lights must be used on any pleasure craft that operates from sunset to sunrise or during periods of restricted visibility.

The navigation lights you are required to display depend on the following:

- The **size** of your craft
- If it is non-powered, **sail-driven or power-driven**
- If it is **underway or at anchor**

NAVIGATION LIGHTS

Power-driven pleasure craft must exhibit a **forward masthead light, sidelights and a sternlight.**

Many small boats (such as bow riders and runabouts) typically have a white light affixed to the top of a light pole that can be placed at the stern of the craft. When underway, this all-round light functions as a combined masthead and sternlight, and must be visible in all directions, mounted higher than the boat structure, cockpit or any other obstruction.

MASTHEAD LIGHT 225°

COLOUR: White

ARC: Shows in an unbroken light over an arc of 225 degrees from dead ahead to 22.5 degrees abaft the beam on both sides of the vessel

POSITION: Fore and aft centerline of the boat. The term 'Masthead Light' is a misnomer. More often than not, the light is not on the top of a mast. On motorboats it is often on a short pole on top of the cabin or windshield, or on a pole at the stern of the boat

ALL-ROUND LIGHT 360°

COLOUR: White

ARC: Shows an unbroken light over an arc of the horizon of 360 degrees

POSITION: Must be placed as to be visible from all directions

TOWING LIGHT 135°

COLOUR: Yellow

ARC: Shows an unbroken light over an arc of the horizon of 135 degrees

POSITION: Placed as close as possible to the stern (back) of the boat

PORT SIDELIGHT 112.5°

COLOUR: Red

ARC: Showing an unbroken light over an arc of the horizon of 112.5 degrees and so fixed as to show the light from dead ahead to 22.5 degrees abaft the beam on the port (left) side

POSITION: Forward area of pleasure craft

STARBOARD SIDELIGHT 112.5°

COLOUR: Green

ARC: Showing an unbroken light over an arc of the horizon of 112.5 degrees and so fixed as to show the light from dead ahead to 22.5 degrees abaft the beam on the starboard (right) side

POSITION: Forward area of pleasure craft

STERNLIGHT 135°

COLOUR: White

ARC: Shows an unbroken light over an arc of the horizon of 135 degrees

POSITION: Placed as close as possible to the stern (back) of the boat

POWERBOATS UNDER 12M (39'4") RULE 23

OPTION 1

- 1 masthead light
- Sidelights
- 1 sternlight

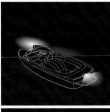

OPTION 2

- 1 all-round white light
- Sidelights

OPTIONAL

- Another masthead light

POWERBOATS FROM 12M (39'4") TO UNDER 50M (164'1") RULE 23

OPTION 1

- 1 masthead light
- Sidelights
- 1 sternlight

OPTIONAL

- Another masthead light

* OPTIONAL – In the Canadian Waters of a roadstead, harbour, river, lake or inland waterway, a sailboat that is also being propelled by a motor may exhibit forward where it can best be seen a conical shape, apex downwards

SAILBOATS UNDER 7M (23') RULE 25

OPTION 1

- Sidelights
- 1 sternlight

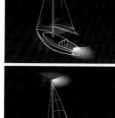

OPTION 2

- 1 lantern, combining the sidelights and sternlight above

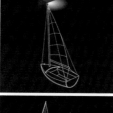

OPTION 3

(If requirements above are not practicable) Have ready at hand an electric torch or lighted lantern showing a white light that you must use far enough in advance to prevent a collision.

OPTIONAL

- 2 all-round lights in a vertical line, the upper being red and the lower green
  *See footnote

SAILBOATS FROM 7M (23') TO UNDER 20M (65'7") RULE 25

OPTION 1

- Sidelights
- 1 sternlight

OPTION 2

- 1 lantern, combining the sidelights and sternlight above

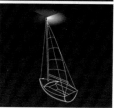

OPTIONAL

- 2 all-round lights in a vertical line, the upper being red and the lower green
  *See footnote

SAILBOATS 20M (65'7") AND OVER RULE 25

OPTION 1

- Sidelights
- 1 sternlight

OPTIONAL

- 2 all-round lights in a vertical line, the upper being red and the lower green
  *See footnote

HUMAN-POWERED BOATS RULE 25

OPTION 1

- Electric torch or lighted lantern showing a white light that you must use far enough in advance to prevent a collision

OPTION 2

- Same lights as listed for sailboats, according to length

OPTIONAL

- Another masthead light

* OPTIONAL – In the Canadian Waters of a roadstead, harbour, river, lake or inland waterway, a sailboat that is also being propelled by a motor may exhibit forward where it can best be seen a conical shape, apex downwards

BOATS AT ANCHOR UNDER 7M (23') RULE 30

OPTION 1

If the boat is in or near a narrow channel, fairway or anchorage, or where other boats normally navigate:

- 1 all-round white light (at night)
- 1 ball (during the day)

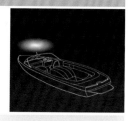

OPTIONAL

- Another all-round white light

BOATS AT ANCHOR FROM 7M (23') TO UNDER 50M (164'1") RULE 30

OPTION 1

- 1 all-round white light (at night) or
- 1 ball (during the day)

OPTIONAL

- Another all-round white light

SPECIAL CIRCUMSTANCES

SEARCH AND RESCUE (SAR) VESSELS

When responding to emergencies, search and rescue vessels, as well as police and government vessels, exhibit blue light(s). You should steer well clear of a vessel with a **blue flashing light.**

WHEN TOWING

If towing another vessel from your stern, you must show:

- Sidelights and a sternlight
- One yellow towing sternlight
- Two masthead lights in a vertical line

If being towed, you must exhibit:

- Sidelights and a sternlight
- A diamond shape
- If you do not have sidelights you must exhibit two aids to navigation, one each at fore and aft

When a boat that doesn't normally tow other boats is engaged in towing, it must display the regular navigation lights and indicate the nature of the relationship between the towing boat and the boat being towed (such as illuminating the towline).

VESSELS BEING PUSHED

When using a powerboat to push another vessel ahead or tow alongside, you must exhibit:

- Two masthead lights in a vertical line, sidelights and a sternlight

BC 4321

POLICE

HEAD-ON APPROACH

If you meet a vessel and see a green, red and white light, you are approaching another power-driven vessel head-on. In this situation **neither vessel has the right-of-way.** Both operators must take early and substantial action to steer well clear of the other vessel. Both operators should reduce their speed and steer to starboard.

If you meet a vessel and see a green and red light but no masthead (white) light, then you are approaching a sail-driven vessel. You are the **give-way craft** and must yield right-of-way to the sailing vessel.

PORT (LEFT) APPROACH

If a green and a white light are visible, then another craft is approaching you from the port (left) side. In this situation, you are the **stand-on craft** and should **maintain** your speed and course. The other craft should take early and substantial action to steer well clear of your craft.

SAFE BOATING TIP

A simple way to decipher powerboat navigation lights is to remember:

If you see a GREEN LIGHT you can 'GO':
Another boat is approaching from your port side

If you see a RED LIGHT you should 'STOP':
Another boat is approaching from your starboard side

UNLOCK INTERACTIVE CONTENT

Scan this page

A detailed look at nighttime navigation.

STARBOARD (RIGHT) APPROACH

If a red and a white light are visible, then another craft is approaching you from the starboard (right) side. In this situation you are the **give-way craft** and must **yield right-of-way**. You should take early and substantial action to steer well clear of the other craft. Reduce your speed, change direction and pass at a safe distance behind the other boat.

WHAT ELSE DOES A WHITE LIGHT INDICATE?

If you see a white light on its own it indicates that you **DO NOT have the right-of-way**. The white light will be identifying one of the following three things:

01 YOU ARE APPROACHING ANOTHER CRAFT FROM BEHIND

If only a white light is visible, you may be approaching another craft from behind. You are the give-way-craft and must take early and substantial action to steer well clear by altering your course and passing at a safe distance on the starboard (right) or port (left) side.

UNLOCK INTERACTIVE CONTENT

Scan this page

See what lights you need to know when navigating at night.

02 YOU ARE APPROACHING A NON-POWERED CRAFT

If you are approaching a non-powered craft, you are the **give-way craft** and must yield the right of way. You should take early and substantial action to **stay well clear** and pass at a safe speed and distance.

Remember that if you're operating a non-powered craft at night, you are required to have **ready for use** an electric torch, flashlight or lighted lantern showing a white light (this rule applies if the boat cannot be equipped with standard navigation lights).

03 YOU ARE APPROACHING AN ANCHORED CRAFT AT NIGHT

If you are approaching an anchored craft, the anchored craft will be exhibiting an all-round white light to indicate to other boaters that their craft is at anchor.

Remember anchored boats should never display their green and red sidelights as these lights will indicate to other boaters that your craft is underway.

LOCK NAVIGATION

A lock is a physical structure of gates that enables vessels to travel between two bodies of water that are of different elevations.

Boats enter the lock from one body of water (vessels may enter from each end of the lock but from only one end at a time). Once the gates at the entrance of the lock are closed, the water level within the lock is increased or decreased to match the elevation of the adjoining body of water. When the correct water level has been reached within the lock, the gates are opened and boats are able to travel onwards.

A restricted speed zone is typically found at the entrance to each side of the lock. **Obey posted speed limits and watch your wake when approaching a lock.** Certain activities such as swimming, fishing, and water-skiing may also be restricted near locks.

ENTERING AND EXITING A LOCK

Operators should always control their speed when in the vicinity of a lock. When approaching a lock you should:

- Identify and adjust for water currents and other boat traffic
- Be aware of and operate according to any posted navigational aids (markers and buoys)
- Identify and adjust for adverse weather conditions such as high wind
- Be prepared for oncoming traffic such as boats exiting the lock

By mooring at the 'blue line' area at the mouth of the lock, the lockmaster is made aware of your intention to enter the lock at the next opening. The lockmaster may provide specific instructions to your vessel including when to enter, in what order and where to moor your vessel once inside the lock. **Only tie up to the 'blue line' if you wish passage through the lock.**

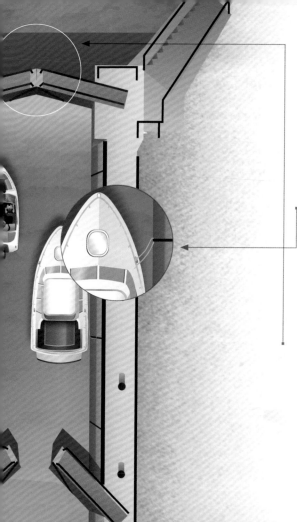

WHEN ENTERING A LOCK

10 MAX km/h

STEP 1

Wait for any instruction from the lockmaster or waterway personnel.

STEP 2

Proceed slowly (maximum speed limit is 10 km/h) and with caution into the lock.
Have crew members posted at the bow and stern of the boat with mooring lines ready to use.

STEP 3

Use the vertical 'drop cables', affixed to the walls of the lock to secure your bow and stern.
Your boat's mooring lines should be **wrapped loosely** around the lock's drop cables allowing for upward or downward movement of your craft. **Never tie your vessel lines to the drop cables.**

STEP 4

Once positioned, turn off all engines, cease from using any fuel-burning appliances, and refrain from smoking. Turn on your engine ventilation system. **Do not leave your mooring lines unattended.**

STEP 5

Once the water level within the lock has reached the proper elevation, the opposite end of the lock will open. The lockmaster will instruct you when to start your engine and when to proceed.

STEP 6

Proceed with caution. Never block the entrance to the lock from other boats that may be entering or exiting.

RIVER NAVIGATION

Operating a pleasure craft or PWC on a river is different than operating on an open waterway. A river presents its own unique hazards and conditions. Some rivers may exhibit strong currents, which can affect your boat's steering and the predictability of your craft. The water level in a river may also rise or lower more rapidly than an open waterway—exposing trees, rocks, sunken islands and other hazards. Always watch for these types of hazards and the navigation aids that may indicate their position.

REMEMBER:

When approaching a blind turn or a narrow channel, always keep as far to the starboard (right) side of waterway as is safe. Power-driven craft and sailboats less than 20 m in length must give way to less manoeuverable crafts while navigating on a river.

If two vessels approach each other in a narrow channel where tide, river flow, or underwater features create dangerous currents, then the vessel going downstream is automatically afforded the right-of-way.

KEEP TO STARBOARD

CANAL NAVIGATION

Canals are man-made waterways. A canal is typically narrower than a channel, and differs from a river as the depth of the water can be controlled.

You should always keep to the starboard (right) side of a channel, particularly when approaching oncoming traffic or entering a blind turn. Power-driven craft and sailboats less than 20 m in length must give way to less manoeuverable crafts operating in a canal or shipping lane. Keep in mind that large vessels, such as commercial ships, are often restricted in their ability to manoeuver in narrow channels and pleasure craft operators should steer well clear.

There are a number of activities that are prohibited while in a canal:

- No excessive noise between 11 pm and 6 am
- No mooring a vessel to a navigation aid
- No fishing within 10 m of a lock or from a bridge that passes over a navigation channel
- It is illegal to dive, jump, scuba-dive, swim or bathe within 40 m of a lock, gate or dam

SAFETY AROUND DAMS

Use caution when near canal dams where currents and undertows can be dangerous. Steer well clear of dams and adjust your course to avoid strong currents near dams, especially when operating a small craft.

SHIPPING LANES

The *Collision Regulations* require that boaters be aware of shipping lanes (traffic lanes) and use extreme caution when near vessel traffic lanes. Large commercial ships often cannot see small pleasure craft operating ahead of them from the bridge. You should always proceed in the appropriate traffic lane in the general direction of traffic flow for that lane. Boaters should join or leave a traffic lane at its termination, but when joining or leaving from either side you should do so at as small an angle to the general direction of traffic flow as practicable.

You should avoid crossing traffic lanes but if you must, cross at a right angle to the general direction of traffic flow. If navigating near a shipping lane or near the termination of a shipping lane you should use caution and avoid the lane with as wide a margin as practicable. Always avoid anchoring in a shipping lane or near its termination. To increase your visibility to larger vessels in or near a shipping lane, you should stay in groups with other small boats, if possible.

LESS MANOEUVRABLE VESSELS

When operating in the vicinity of large commercial vessels, remember that these vessels have limited visibility, turning and stopping capabilities.

The *Collision Regulations* require that **all smaller pleasure craft less than 20 m in length (including sailboats) must give right-of-way to larger, less manoeuverable vessels.** This is one of a few instances in which a motorized vessel has the right-of-way over a non-powered vessel.

Large vessels, those towing a barge and those engaged in fishing activities with nets and trawls always have the right-of-way and are considered to be the **stand-on craft.** Pleasure powerboats and sailboats must take early and substantial action to stay well clear of these types of vessels.

REMEMBER:
The *Collision Regulations* require that pleasure sailing craft and power-driven vessels less than 20 m in length shall not hinder the passage of power-driven vessels which can safely navigate only in a narrow channel or those craft that are navigating in a traffic lane.

NAVIGATING AT SEA

Boaters are required to follow the International Regulations for preventing collisions at sea and the Canadian modifications upon the high seas and in all waters connected therewith and navigable by vessels as described in the *Collision Regulations* Rules 1 and 2 and the *Canada Shipping Act 2001* Section 562. For more information visit www.tc.gc.ca.

When traveling to the United States by sea or inland waterway, Canadian citizens are required to present a single document that complies with the Western Hemisphere Travel Initiative (WHTI). These requirements came into effect on June 1, 2009. Boaters should check with the U.S. Department of Homeland Security for up-to-date requirements.

MODULE 5 SUMMARY

Understanding and abiding by navigation and right-of-way rules is essential for safe boating. Remember that certain types and sizes of craft are governed by different navigation rules under the *Collision Regulations*. Knowing what actions to take when approaching another craft will help you reduce the risk of collision and injury to yourself and others. Always keep a lookout for other boat traffic, relative to your sectors of navigation.

You should be able to navigate with confidence during periods of restricted visibility, such as when operating at night or during poor weather conditions. Being able to recognize different types of craft by the configuration of their navigation lights is vital for safe operation during such conditions.

By completing this module you should know the rules and regulations for operating on unique waterways such as canals, rivers and locks. Remember that less manoeuverable vessels have the right-of-way when operating in shipping lanes and confined waterways, such as rivers and canals.

MODULE 5 QUIZ

1   YOU ARE APPROACHING ANOTHER CRAFT AFTER SUNSET AND SEE A WHITE LIGHT. WHAT SHOULD YOU DO?

A   Immediately stop–you are approaching a boat that is in distress
B   Continue your same course and speed
C   Slow down and proceed with caution – you are approaching a non-powered boat, a boat that is at anchor or another boat from the stern
D   Speed up and overtake the boat–you are approaching a boat from the stern

2   DO BOATS INVOLVED IN FISHING ACTIVITIES, SUCH AS THOSE TRAWLING WITH NETS, HAVE RIGHT-OF-WAY OVER NON-POWERED CRAFT?

A   Yes
B   No
C   Only in large bodies of water
D   Only at night

3   WHAT ACTIONS SHOULD YOU TAKE IF OVERTAKING ANOTHER POWER-DRIVEN VESSEL?

A   You are the give-way craft and if possible pass on the starboard side
B   You are the give-way craft and if possible pass on the port side
C   You have the right of way and can pass on either side you want
D   You should not pass and just wait until they change direction

MODULE 5 QUIZ

4   WHICH OF THE FOLLOWING GOVERNS NAVIGATION RULES ON CANADIAN WATERWAYS?

A   The *Small Vessel Regulations*
B   The *Collision Regulations*
C   The *Charts and Nautical Publications Regulations*
D   The *Contraventions Act*

5   THE TERM 'RESTRICTED VISIBILITY' APPLIES BEST TO WHICH OF THE FOLLOWING WEATHER CONDITIONS?

A   Heavy boat traffic
B   Haze on a hot day
C   Darkness or fog
D   Bright sunlight

6   WHAT IS THE STAND-ON CRAFT?

A   The craft that has the right-of-way
B   The craft that does not have the right-of-way
C   A craft that is at anchor
D   A craft that is slowing down

7   WHICH THREE COLOURS ARE USED FOR NAVIGATION LIGHTS?

A   Red, green and blue
B   Red, green and yellow
C   Green, red and white
D   White, blue and yellow

8   ACCORDING TO THE COLLISION REGULATIONS, WHAT SHOULD YOU DO IF ANOTHER POWERBOAT APPROACHES YOU FROM THE PORT SIDE?

A   Maintain your course and speed with caution
B   Immediately steer to starboard
C   Speed up and pass in front of the other boat
D   Steer well clear of the other boat

9   WHEN ANCHORING FOR THE NIGHT WHAT LIGHT(S) SHOULD YOU DISPLAY?

A   Red and green sidelight
B   All-round white light
C   Red and green sidelights and all-round light
D   White stern light

10 YOU ARE APPROACHING ANOTHER CRAFT AFTER SUNSET AND SEE A GREEN AND WHITE LIGHT. WHAT ACTION SHOULD YOU TAKE?

A   The other craft is approaching from the port side—use caution and maintain your speed and direction
B   Immediately alter your course and pass in front of the other craft
C   Immediately alter your course and pass behind the other craft
D   Stop and signal the other craft to change direction

module 6
MARKERS AND BUOYS

AIDS TO NAVIGATION

'Aids to Navigation' are **the system of buoys and markers that assist a boater in determining his or her position** and identify any potential dangers and waterway obstructions. External to pleasure craft, Aids to Navigation can be used to plot position and course on nautical charts and other nautical publications. Aids to Navigation also assist the pleasure craft operator in choosing the most preferred and safest route.

It is prohibited under the *Criminal Code of Canada* to interfere with any navigation aid. Operators should never tie up to a marker, buoy or any other aid to navigation. In addition, no person may willfully alter, remove or conceal a signal, buoy or other type of navigation marker.

Two main systems of navigation are used on Canadian Waterways: the **Lateral System** and the **Cardinal System**. All Aids to Navigation have identifying marks such as colours, lights and numbers.

WHAT IS A BUOY?

A buoy is a floating marker or signal which is affixed to the bottom of the waterway or mounted on a feature (such as an island) of the waterway.

Buoys serve 4 main functions:

- Provide warnings
- Provide information
- Mark underwater hazards
- Provide a system for navigation

FLOATING BUOYS

There are different styles of floating buoys used on Canadian waterways:

PILLAR BUOYS   SPAR BUOYS   CANS (GREEN)   NUNS (RED)

- **PILLAR BUOYS:** Pillar Buoys are typically the largest of all floating buoys and will sometimes have a lighted top. These types of buoys tend to be narrower than Can and Nun buoys
- **SPAR BUOYS:** Spar Buoys are common on smaller waterways. They have a cylinder shape and are typically smaller than Light Buoys.
- **CAN BUOYS:** Can buoys are wider than Spar Buoys. They are always green in colour and should be kept on the left (port) side when heading upstream.
- **NUN/CONICAL BUOYS:** Nun buoys are also wider than spar buoys. They are always red in colour and should be kept on the right (starboard) side when heading upstream.

All floating buoys are affixed to the bottom of the waterway using a structure of underwater cables and anchors.

SYSTEMS OF BUOYS IN CANADA

THERE ARE SEVERAL SYSTEMS OF BUOYS AND MARKERS USED ON
CANADIAN WATERWAYS TO AID IN NAVIGATION:

> ### 01 THE LATERAL SYSTEM
> The Lateral System consists of red and green buoys used to mark
> preferred safe routes. The Lateral System also includes Fairway Buoys,
> Isolated Danger Buoys and Day Beacons.

> ### 02 CARDINAL SYSTEM
> The Cardinal System consists of yellow and black buoys that
> indicate safe routes by the cardinal compass points.

> ### 03 SPECIAL PURPOSE BUOYS
> Special Purpose Buoys may be yellow or white in colour and are
> used to mark dangers such as (but not limited to) racecourses,
> underwater structures, pipelines, etc.

01 THE LATERAL SYSTEM

The Lateral System is used to mark the **most preferred and safest routes.** Consisting of **red** and **green** buoys, this system marks the course of deepest water and indicates on which side of the buoy you should safely pass.

In the Lateral System, buoys and beacons indicate the sides of the channel or route relative to a conventional direction of buoyage (usually upstream). They also mark junctions (a point where two channels meet) or bifurcations (the point where a channel divides). They can also mark a place where two tributaries meet.

Keep in mind: when navigating along the course of a channel or fairway you should be as near to the outer limit of the channel or fairway on the starboard side as is safely possible.

There are two main types of Lateral System buoys which are most familiar to boaters and are standard for international waterways:

* RED STARBOARD-HAND BUOYS
* GREEN PORT-HAND BUOYS

In total, there are six types of lateral buoys including:

* Starboard-hand Buoys
* Port-hand Buoys
* Starboard Bifurcation Buoys
* Port Bifurcation Buoys
* Fairway Buoys
* Isolated Danger Buoys

SAFE BOATING TIP

Remember: opposites attract when heading upstream! Your boat's green sidelight will always match up with any red buoy that your boat approaches when heading upstream, and your red starboard sidelight will always pair with any green buoy that your boat approaches when heading upstream. Red/green, green/red!

HAND BUOYS

AB82

NT17

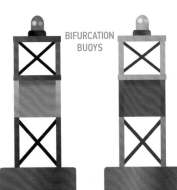

BIFURCATION BUOYS

FAIRWAY BUOYS

N

ISOLATED DANGER BUOYS

STARBOARD-HAND BUOYS

Starboard-Hand Buoys are **red** in colour and mark the **right side of a channel** or the location of a specific danger. Starboard-Hand Buoys must be kept on the **right-hand side** of your boat when heading **upstream**.

Starboard-Hand Buoys are identified by letter(s) and even-digit number(s), and in standard configuration, are pointed on the top. If they do not have a red light they will be conical on the top.

Starboard-Hand Buoys may also be fitted with a red light that flashes in either a:

- Fl pattern (single flashes in four second intervals); or
- Q pattern (quick, single flashes one second apart)

PORT-HAND BUOYS

Port-Hand Buoys are **green** in colour and mark the **left side of a channel** or the location of a specific danger. Port-Hand Buoys must be kept on the **left-hand side** of your boat when heading **upstream**.

Port-Hand Buoys are identified by letter(s) and odd-digit number(s), and in standard configuration, are flat on the top. In some instances, a Port-Hand Buoy may be fitted with a top-mark consisting of a single green cylinder.

Port-Hand Buoys may also be fitted with a green light that flashes in either a:

- Fl pattern (single flashes in four second intervals); or
- Q pattern (quick single flashes one second apart)

BIFURCATION BUOYS

Part of the Lateral System, Bifurcation Buoys indicate the junction of two or more channels. You may pass on either side of these buoys when proceeding upstream but the preferred channel is indicated by the colour of the topmost band:

STARBOARD-JUNCTION BIFURCATION BUOY

Starboard-Junction Bifurcation Buoys are red in colour with a green horizontal band at the midsection. Starboard-Junction Buoys should be kept on the starboard (right) side of the vessel when navigating upstream.

PORT-JUNCTION BIFURCATION BUOY

Port-Junction Bifurcation Buoys are green in colour with a red horizontal band at the midsection. Port-Junction Buoys should be kept on the port (left) side of the vessel when navigating upstream.

FAIRWAY BUOYS

Fairway Buoys are used to mark the **entrance to a channel, the centre of a shipping channel or a safe approach to land**. Operators should keep the Fairway Buoy on the left (port) side whether proceeding upstream or downstream.

Fairway Buoys are identified by the following:

- Red and white in colour, divided vertically with one red side and one white side
- Will have a ball shaped top-mark
- May be equipped with a white light that flashes in a Mo(A) sequence – one short flash, followed by one long flash repeated ten times per minute

ISOLATED DANGER BUOYS

An Isolated Danger Buoy is used to mark an **isolated hazard** or obstruction such as a rock, shoal or sunken island. **The buoy will be moored on, or above, an isolated danger that has navigable (i.e. safe) water all around it.** You should refer to a marine chart to determine the features of the isolated danger (i.e. size, depth, exact location etc.) and should navigate well clear of the marked danger.

Isolated Danger Buoys are identified by the following:

- Black in colour with a wide red band at the midpoint
- A top-mark consisting of two black balls
- May be equipped with a white light that flashes in a FL(2) sequence – a two flash sequence repeated every four seconds

DAY BEACONS

Day Beacons are signs posted on land or water. They are without lights and are intended for daytime use only. Day Beacons use the same colours as the Lateral System and are typically used as channel or hazard markers. They may be marked with reflective lettering for identification on marine charts.

PORT-HAND DAY BEACON:

A Port-Hand Day Beacon consists of a black and green square on a white background framed by a reflective green border. A Port-Hand Day Beacon **identifies the port (left) side of a channel or hazard and must be kept on the left side when proceeding upstream.** Port-Hand Day Beacons may display an odd number marked with reflective white lettering for reference on marine charts.

STARBOARD-HAND DAY BEACON:

A Starboard-Hand Day Beacon consists of a red triangle on a white background framed by a reflective red border. A Starboard-Hand Day Beacon **identifies the starboard (right) side of the channel** or hazard and **must be kept on the right side when proceeding upstream.** Starboard-Hand Day Beacons may display an even number marked with reflective white lettering for reference on marine charts.

PORT-JUNCTION DAY BEACON:

A Port-Junction Day Beacon marks the **junction of two channels** and may be passed on either side. If the preferred channel is desired, the Port-Junction Day Beacon should be kept on the vessel's port (left) side when travelling upstream.

STARBOARD-JUNCTION DAY BEACON:

A Starboard-Junction Day Beacon marks the **junction of two channels** and may be passed on either side. If the preferred channel is desired, the Starboard-Junction Day Beacon should be kept on the vessel's starboard (right) side when travelling upstream.

'RED RIGHT RETURNING'

Many boaters are not certain on which side of a marker buoy they should pass. A simple way to remember is to use the 'Red Right Returning' memory aid:

'Red Right Returning' refers to keeping the red starboard-hand buoy on the right side of your boat when:

- Returning to harbor
- Heading upstream
- Entering a channel from seaward

UNLOCK INTERACTIVE CONTENT

Scan this page

Which way is upstream? Scan this page and find out how to tell!

HOW DO I DETERMINE WHICH WAY IS UPSTREAM?

Travelling upstream means you are travelling **against the current**. In many places, the direction of the current is determined by consensus or by the tide. Although not always the case, often you'll find that water flows from north to south–this means that if you're going north, you will likely be heading upstream. To help you determine the direction of water flow, use the following tips:

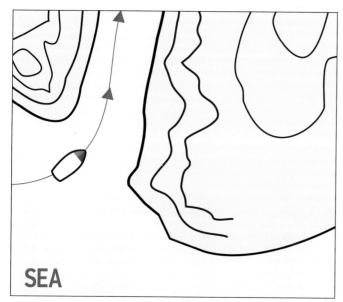

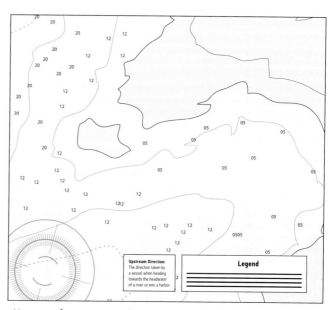

- If you're entering a channel from the sea, you are considered to be travelling 'upstream'

- You can refer to a marine chart to identify the upstream direction of travel

02 THE CARDINAL SYSTEM

The Cardinal System consists of yellow and black buoys that are used to assist boaters in identifying the **location of safe water**. Safe water lies on the north, south, east or west side of the buoys. For example, a North Cardinal Buoy indicates that safe water lies to the north of the buoy. Cardinal Buoys may be equipped with a light and/or letters for identification on a marine chart. **Remember: with Cardinal Buoys, the safest water lies in the direction indicated by the buoy. Water in the opposite direction should be considered unsafe and avoided.**

Cardinal markers are spar or pillar-shaped (with a flat top). The position of the yellow and black colour bands indicates the cardinal compass points of north, south, east or west and therefore the direction of the safest water. If so equipped, top-marks consisting of two cones indicate the direction of safe water.

NORTH   SOUTH   EAST   WEST

NORTH CARDINAL BUOY   SOUTH CARDINAL BUOY   EAST CARDINAL BUOY   WEST CARDINAL BUOY

CARDINAL BUOYS AND THEIR SIGNAL LIGHTS

NORTH CARDINAL BUOY

PURPOSE: A North Cardinal Buoy is positioned so that the safest water lies to the north of the buoy

COLOUR: Black on the top and yellow on the bottom

LIGHT: North flashes once

SOUTH CARDINAL BUOY

PURPOSE: A South Cardinal Buoy is positioned so that the safest water lies to the south of the buoy

COLOUR: Yellow on the top and black on the bottom

LIGHT: South flashes in a group of six times followed by one long flash

EAST CARDINAL BUOY

PURPOSE: An East Cardinal Buoy is positioned so that the safest water lies to the east of the buoy

COLOUR: Black with a wide yellow band around the midsection

LIGHT: East flashes in a group three times

WEST CARDINAL BUOY

PURPOSE: A West Cardinal Buoy is positioned so that the safest water lies to the west of the buoy

COLOUR: Yellow with a wide black band around the midsection

LIGHT: West flashes in a group nine times

BOATING RESTRICTION SIGNS

Boating Restriction Signs are framed in orange and the symbol on the sign indicates the type of restriction that applies. If the sign is arrow shaped, the restriction applies in the direction pointed by the arrow. Signs with a green border indicate that a special condition applies to the restriction. Be aware of the restrictions that are local to your boating area.

01 Standarized speed limit

02 No power-driven vessels or vessels driven by electrical propulsion in the direction of the arrow

03 No internal combustion engine permitted

04 No vessels permitted

05 Engine power limit

06 No skiing north of the sign

07 No power-driven vessels or vessels driven by electric propulsion during the hours and days in red

SAFE BOATING TIP

This boating restriction sign indicates that **power-driven vessels or vessels powered by electric propulsion are prohibited from entering the area**.

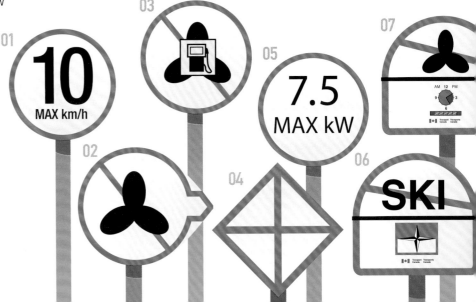

03 SPECIAL BUOYS AND FLAGS

Operators must be able to identify the variety of special buoys and flags as they mark specific hazards and provide information to the operator. These markers may be equipped with lights and may be marked with letters or numbers for marine chart identification.

DIVING BUOY:

SWIMMING BUOY:

KEEP OUT BUOY:

Diving Buoys mark an area where scuba diving (or other such diving activities) are taking place.

- White in colour
- **Carries a red flag not less than 50 cm square with a white diagonal stripe**

Swimming Buoys mark the perimeter of swimming areas.

- White in colour
- Yellow light may flash in 4-second sequence

Keep Out Buoys mark an area of water where boating is prohibited.

- White in colour with an orange diamond containing an orange cross on two opposite sides and two orange horizontal bands, one above and one below the diamond symbols
- Yellow light may flash in 4-second sequence

CONTROL BUOY:

INFORMATION BUOY:

HAZARD BUOY:

Control Buoys mark an area of water where boating is restricted.

- White, with an orange, open-faced circle on two opposite sides and two horizontal orange bands, one above and below the circles. A black symbol inside the orange circles indicates the type of restriction in effect
- Yellow light may flash in 4-second sequence

Information Buoys provide information of interest to boaters using words or symbols.

- White, with an orange, open-faced square symbol on two opposite sides and two orange horizontal bands, one above and one below the square symbol
- Yellow light may flash in 4-second sequence

Hazard Buoys mark random hazards such as rocks or shoals.

- White, with an orange diamond symbol on two opposite sides and two orange horizontal bands one above and one below the diamond
- Yellow light may flash in 4-second sequence

CAUTIONARY BUOY:

ANCHORAGE BUOY:

MOORING BUOY:

Cautionary Buoys mark dangers such as underwater structures, areas where no safe channel exists or may mark traffic separations.

- Yellow in colour
- Identification letters displayed
- May carry a top mark that is a single yellow 'X' shape
- Yellow light may flash in 4-second sequence

Anchorage Buoys identify areas where it is safe to anchor.

- Yellow with a symbol representing an anchor
- Sometimes identified by letters
- Yellow light may flash in 4-second sequence

Mooring Buoys are the only Aid to Navigation that you can legally secure your boat to.

- White in colour with an orange top

MODULE 6 SUMMARY

In this module you learned about Aids to Navigation and the different systems of markers and buoys in Canada. Markers and buoys indicate the most preferred and safest routes for navigation and also mark specific hazards and/or dangers. Keep in mind that you can reference markers and buoys on marine charts by their location and the numbers marked on them.

The Lateral System is the most common system of buoys in Canada and consists of green Port-hand Buoys and red Starboard-hand Buoys. Don't forget 'Red Right Returning', the memory aid which refers to keeping the red Starboard-hand Buoys on the right side when returning upstream into harbour or headwaters. You will need to determine upstream and downstream directions for the specific waterway on which you will be operating in order to navigate successfully using the Lateral System. You should be confident of these rules before heading out on any waterway.

The Cardinal System marks safe water according to the Compass points of north, south, east and west. You should be able to identify and navigate according to the Cardinal Buoy system.

Special Buoys and flags mark specific hazards and/or provide important information to boaters. These include Hazard Buoys, Control Buoys, Information Buoys, Anchorage Buoys, Swimming Buoys, Diving Buoys and others. You should be able to recognize these buoys and operate safely in their vicinity.

MODULE 6 QUIZ

1   WHAT IS THE PURPOSE OF A BIFURCATION BUOY?

A   Identifies an isolated danger
B   Marks a head dam
C   Marks the junction of two or more channels
D   Used to signal a 'diver-down'

2   IF YOU APPROACH A JUNCTION DAY BEACON WHILE BOATING, WHAT IS THAT SIGN MARKING FOR YOU?

A   A protected environmental zone where only boats 10 hp and under may enter
B   A point where the channel divides and the preferred direction for boaters to take
C   The intersection of a shipping lane and a commercial lane where boat traffic is limited
D   The entrance to a military port area where boat operation is highly restricted

3   WHICH ONE OF THE FOLLOWING IS THE CORRECT DESCRIPTION OF A PORT-HAND BUOY?

A   Red in colour and indicates the right side of a channel
B   Black and red in colour and indicates the junction of channels
C   Red and white in colour and indicates a safe approach to harbour
D   Green in colour and indicates the left side of a channel

MODULE 6 QUIZ

4   WHAT ACTION SHOULD YOU TAKE IF YOU SEE A SERIES OF WHITE BUOYS?

A   Speed up and leave the designated area
B   Steer well clear as the buoy is marking an underwater hazard
C   Steer well clear as the buoys are marking a swimming area
D   You are approaching a restricted mooring area

5   CAUTIONARY BUOYS ARE WHAT COLOUR?

A   Black and yellow
B   Red
C   Yellow
D   Blue with a white diagonal stripe

6   CARDINAL BUOYS ARE USED TO IDENTIFY WHICH OF THE FOLLOWING?

A   Persons engaged in diving activities
B   Safe water on the North, South, East or West side of the buoy
C   Specific hazards such as submerged power lines
D   A safe anchorage area

7   WHAT COLOUR IS A SWIMMING BUOY?

A   White
B   Red
C   Orange
D   Blue

8   YOU SEE A BUOY THAT IS WHITE IN COLOUR WITH TWO HORIZONTAL ORANGE BANDS AND AN ORANGE DIAMOND. WHAT TYPE OF BUOY ARE YOU APPROACHING?

A   Cautionary Buoy
B   Anchorage Buoy
C   Control Buoy
D   Hazard Buoy

9   YOU ARE HEADING UPSTREAM AND APPROACH A BUOY THAT IS GREEN IN COLOUR. WHAT ACTION SHOULD YOU TAKE?

A   Stop and proceed in the opposite direction
B   Proceed while keeping the buoy on the right side of your craft
C   Proceed while keeping the buoy on the left side of your craft
D   Use caution and pass as far from the buoy as possible

10   WHAT IS THE PURPOSE OF A CONTROL BUOY?

A   Provides information of interest to boaters
B   Indicates speed limits
C   Marks an area where boating is prohibited
D   Marks an area where boating is restricted

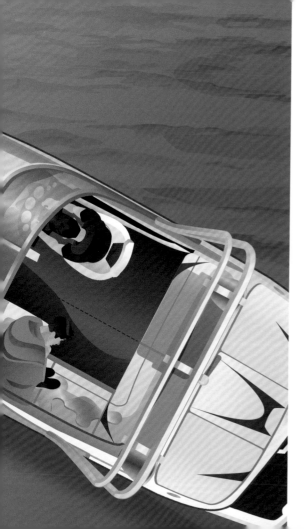

module 7
EMERGENCY PREPAREDNESS

BOATING EMERGENCIES

Boating emergencies can come in various forms and degrees of severity. The key to safe, enjoyable boating is being prepared and having the right knowledge. You may not be able to predict the unexpected–but you can prepare for it.

In a boating emergency you should:

- Remain calm
- Properly **assess the situation** and then take appropriate action
- Ensure your own safety and that of your passengers
- If necessary, signal your need for help using a **recognized distress signal**

WHAT TO DO IN AN EMERGENCY

Remembering the following will help you respond effectively in an emergency:

- Always ensure that everyone onboard is wearing a PFD or life jacket
- The *Small Vessel Regulations* require that certain vessels carry an emergency kit (keep the proper equipment and supplies onboard to stop hull leaks and make minor on-water repairs)
- Carry a first aid kit onboard at all times
- If you or any of your passengers have been injured: whoever is closest to the injured person should assess the victim's breathing and administer first aid if necessary

RENDERING ASSISTANCE—IT'S THE LAW!

REMEMBER:

Always keep a lookout for other boaters signalling distress and/or need of assistance. If you have witnessed a distress signal or an emergency situation, you are **required by law** to help other boaters as long as it is safe to do so.

SAFE BOATING TIP

Would you know how to perform rescue breathing techniques in an emergency? Have you ever treated a person suffering from hypothermia? If you don't know how to handle these types of emergencies you should take a first aid course. If an emergency arises, you'll be able to respond quickly—you may even be able to prevent permanent injury or death.

IF YOUR CRAFT HAS RUN AGROUND

STEP 1

Determine whether passengers and the vessel are in danger.

STEP 2

Immediately shift the motor to neutral.

STEP 3

Visually and/or verbally confirm that all passengers are present and accounted for.

STEP 4

Ensure that everyone is wearing a PFD or life jacket.

STEP 5

Determine if there are other craft in the vicinity that may offer assistance.

STEP 6

Determine if there is any danger of being hit by other boat traffic.

STEP 7

Inspect the hull and equipment for any damage. Check for rising or accumulating water in the hull.

STEP 8

If the hull is undamaged, assess your course of action:

- Is it possible to dislodge the craft from its obstruction?
- Is it necessary to lighten the craft by removing equipment and passengers?
- Is it possible that passengers may be able to carefully push the craft off the obstruction?
- Is it possible to use the reverse thrust of the engine to free the craft from the obstruction without revving the engine?

STEP 9

If necessary, signal your need for help using a recognized distress signal.

ALWAYS KNOW YOUR BOAT'S DRAFT TO AVOID RUNNING AGROUND

DRAFT

SAFE BOATING TIP

Your first reaction when running aground might be to rev the engine in reverse in an effort to dislodge your craft—this is the one thing you should not do. You could damage your boat's rudder or propeller. You might also suck sand or mud into your engine's cooling system.

Always consult a marine chart for the area in which you'll be operating. Being aware of the water depth and the draft that your boat requires will ensure you can avoid running aground and damaging your propeller.

IF YOUR CRAFT HAS CAPSIZED

STEP 1

Ensure that everyone is wearing a PFD or life jacket.

STEP 2

Visually and/or verbally confirm that all passengers are present and accounted for.

STEP 3

Determine if there are other craft in the vicinity that may offer assistance.

STEP 4

Determine if there is any danger of being hit by other boat traffic. **If you and your passengers are far from shore or unable to reach shore, stay with your craft. If your craft is not fully submerged, climb onto the overturned hull.** This will help you retain energy, increase your survival time in cold weather/water conditions and increase your visibility to other boaters. However, only re-board the capsized vessel if it is still afloat, seaworthy and safe to do so. If it is appropriate to leave the craft (less than 50 m to shore), swim to shore and immediately get assistance.

STEP 5

If necessary, signal your need for help using a recognized distress signal.

SAFE BOATING TIP

If your boat capsizes and you are more than 50 m from shore, don't try to swim for shore!

HULL LEAKS AND FLOODING

Striking underwater hazards such as a submerged rock, sunken island, shoal or deadhead may cause serious damage to your craft resulting in a breach of the hull. If the hull of your craft is breached, leaking and flooding will occur. Improper fitting of the craft's drain plug or a worn or improperly installed exhaust/out-drive seal may also result in flooding.

If you witness water accumulating in the hull of your boat, immediately take the following actions:

STEP 1 Determine whether the passengers and the vessel are in danger.

STEP 2 If the craft is moving bring it to a complete stop (this will reduce water pressure against the hull and reduce the speed at which water is entering the boat). Turn on the bilge pump (if equipped) and identify the source of the leak or flooding.

STEP 3 Stop the hull leak if possible. The use of tapered wooden plugs, a hull patch kit, towel, rag or other malleable material may work.

STEP 4 Attempt to remove accumulations of water. You can remove water by using a hand-held bailer, manual pump or bilge pumping system. You should use a device that suits the circumstances and the type of craft. (Your craft should be equipped with appropriate bailing devices as stipulated by the *Small Vessel Regulations*.)

STEP 5 If necessary, signal your need for help using a recognized distress signal.

REMEMBER:
You should always carry the tools and materials needed to temporarily stop hull leaks or flooding.

These include:

- Tapered wooden plugs
- Hull patch kit
- Towels, rags or other malleable material

IF YOUR CRAFT IS SWAMPED OR IS SINKING

A boat is 'swamped' when it fills with water from over the side. Swamping can be caused by large waves coming over the gunwales or transom of your boat if it has been overloaded. If your boat has been swamped or is sinking:

STEP 1

Ensure that everyone is wearing a PFD or life jacket.

STEP 2

Visually and/or verbally confirm that all passengers are present and accounted for.

STEP 3

Determine if there are other craft in the vicinity that may offer assistance.

STEP 4

Determine if there is any danger of being hit by other boat traffic.

STEP 5

Attempt to stop any hull leaks or flooding if possible.

STEP 6

If you cannot stop your craft from sinking, immediately swim to safety.

STEP 7

Signal your need for help using a recognized distress signal.

BC 4321

COLLISIONS

If your craft has been involved in a collision:

STEP 1

Ensure that everyone is wearing a PFD or life jacket.

STEP 2

Visually and/or verbally confirm that all passengers are present and accounted for.

STEP 3

Determine if there are other craft in the vicinity that may offer assistance.

STEP 4

Determine if there is any danger of being hit by another boat.

STEP 5

Inspect the hull and equipment for any damage—check for rising or accumulating water in the hull.

STEP 6

If necessary, signal your need for assistance.

REPORTING A COLLISION

You are required to take certain actions if you have been involved in a collision:

- ☑ You are required to stop and identify yourself, your vessel, your home port, your ports of origin and destination to the other craft

- ☑ You are required to assist the crew of the other vessel if it is safe to do so

- ☑ If damage exceeding $1,000 has occurred, or the seaworthiness of either vessel has been compromised, you are required by law to file an accident report with the local authorities

- ☑ If serious injury or death has occurred, you are required by law to report the collision to the local law enforcement agency

ABANDONING SHIP

If circumstances (such as an onboard fire) dictate that you and your passengers need to abandon ship, do the following:

STEP 1   Ensure that you and your passengers are wearing a PFD or life jacket

STEP 2   If time permits signal your need for assistance with a radio, flare, horn or flashlight

STEP 3   If possible jump to the windward side of the boat (the boat will drift away from you)

STEP 4   Once in the water swim well clear of the boat

STEP 5   Visually and/or verbally confirm that all passengers are present and accounted for

PERSON OVERBOARD EMERGENCY

Over 40% of all boating fatalities are the result of people falling overboard. You should be prepared with the right knowledge and equipment to rescue a person overboard:

- Ensure that your emergency equipment is **properly maintained** and **readily accessible**

- **Practice overboard rescue techniques with your passengers** and make them aware of their responsibilities

- Practice **manoeuvering** your pleasure craft to **properly position your boat** so that you're ready to perform an overboard rescue if an emergency arises

- Be able to keep in mind the water surface and weather conditions, as well as the condition of the person overboard during a person overboard rescue

RESCUING A PERSON OVERBOARD

First, you should reduce your speed and prepare to turn around:

STEP 1

Immediately throw the person a brightly-coloured, buoyant item such as a life ring or life jacket – this will keep them afloat, increase their visibility in the water and mark their position.

STEP 2

Assign another passenger to keep a lookout of the person overboard and continuously point to the overboard person's location in the water.

STEP 3

Carefully manoeuver the boat **turning the bow into the wind** and in a downwind position from the victim – you want the person overboard to **drift towards your boat**.

STEP 4

Once in rescue position, **shut down the engine to avoid accidental movement and injury** (such as a propeller strike).

THEN, USE ONE OF THE FOLLOWING OVERBOARD RESCUE TECHNIQUES TO RECOVER THE PERSON OVERBOARD:

1. USE A REACHING ASSIST:

- Move to the side of the boat and keep your weight low
- Use the reaching assist to pull the victim to the side of the boat and assist them back into the boat

2. USE A BUOYANT HEAVING LINE:

- Throw the buoyant heaving line so that it lands behind the victim
- Slowly pull the line towards you so the victim can grab onto it
- Pull the victim to the side of the boat and assist them back into the boat

3. USE A LIFE RING:

- Ensure the life ring is secured to the boat with a line
- Throw the life ring so that it lands behind the victim
- Slowly pull the line towards you so the victim is able to grab onto it
- Pull the victim to the side of the boat and assist them back into the boat

SAFE BOATING TIP

Never jump into the water to rescue the person overboard because if they are panicking and thrashing in the water, they could pull you under.

HYPOTHERMIA AND COLD WATER IMMERSION

Hypothermia is a drop in core body temperature, caused by **prolonged exposure to abnormally low temperatures**. Hypothermia can be caused by:

- Immersion in cold water
- Exposure to cold air and wind while in water-soaked clothing
- Prolonged exposure to low water and air temperatures
- Hypothermia sets in when core body tempurature drops below 35.0 degrees Celcius

COLD WATER SHOCK

Even more dangerous is cold water shock, which likely causes more fatalities than hypothermia. Cold water shock occurs when a person experiences sudden, unexpected immersion into water 15° or below. For three to five minutes after sudden immersion in cold water, a person will gasp for breath and may also experience muscle spasms and a rise in heart rate and blood pressure. The instant muscle spasms and gasp reflex can cause the victim to involuntarily ingest water and drown. A rise in heart rate and blood pressure can result in a heart attack or stroke.

1-10-1

1-10-1 is a simple way to remember the first 3 phases of cold water immersion and the approximate time each phase takes.

1- COLD SHOCK:

An initial deep and sudden gasp followed by **hyperventilation and a rise in heart rate.** Cold shock will pass in about one minute. During that time concentrate on avoiding panic and getting control of your breathing. Wearing a life jacket during this phase is critically important to keep you afloat and breathing.

10 - COLD INCAPACITATION:

Over approximately the next 10 minutes, you will lose the effective use of your fingers, arms and legs for any meaningful movement. Swim failure will occur within these critical minutes and if you are in the water without a life jacket, drowning will likely occur.

1- HYPOTHERMIA:

Even in ice water, it could take approximately one hour before becoming unconscious due to hypothermia. You should understand the techniques of how to delay hypothermia, self rescue and calling for help in order to increase your chances of survival.

Cold water can also paralyze your muscles instantly—making it extremely difficult to put on a life jacket or PFD. It is important to remember that cold water shock can occur throughout the year, even during warm summer months when water temperatures can remain lower than outside air temperatures.

STAGES OF HYPOTHERMIA

If suffering from hypothermia, the victim's core body temperature drops below normal levels, resulting in weakened muscular functions, reduced co-ordination and slowing of mental functions.

A person suffering from hypothermia will exhibit progressive symptoms including:

01 EARLY STAGE:

- The victim is still conscious
- Shivering
- Slurred speech

02 INTERMEDIATE STAGE:

- The victim may be irrational, confused and sleepy and will exhibit a lack of co-ordination
- Slow and weak pulse
- Slow breathing
- Shivering will now be slowed or absent

03 FINAL STAGE:

- The victim may lose consciousness
- Weak, irregular or absent pulse
- Weak, irregular or absent breathing

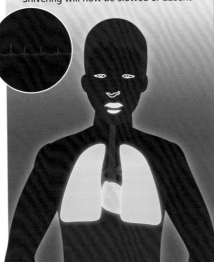

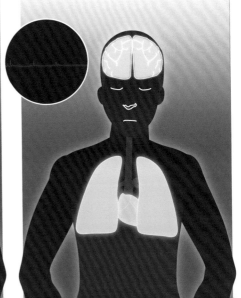

COLD WATER/WEATHER SURVIVAL GEAR

If you plan to operate in the early spring, late fall or in other cold environments, you and your passengers should always make use of cold weather and cold water protection gear. You can protect yourself by wearing a life jacket or PFD and **multiple layers of dry, light clothing and a water or wind proof outer layer.** Gear specifically designed for cold environments offers better protection from the elements and can delay the effects of hypothermia:

- WET SUIT: traps and heats water against the body and should be used with a flotation device
- DRY SUIT: remains dry on the inside and should be used with a flotation device and thermal liner
- SURVIVAL SUIT: helps retain body heat and works as a full body flotation device
- IMMERSION SUIT: to be used in extreme conditions when abandoning a vessel
- EXPOSURE COVERALL: a PFD with thermal protection

Be sure to choose cold weather protection gear that is appropriate to the temperature and your planned operating environment. Knowing how your equipment works in the water is also important. Test your equipment in a warm swimming pool or in calm water before you need it in an emergency.

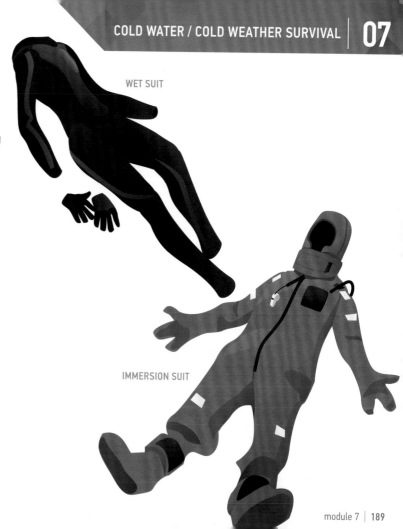

WET SUIT

IMMERSION SUIT

RESCUING A PERSON WITH HYPOTHERMIA

IMMEDIATE ACTIONS:

☐ Ensure that you are wearing an approved PFD or life jacket

☐ Assess the victim's current condition:
What stage of hypothermia is he/she exhibiting?

☐ Clearly identify yourself to the person and ask him/her to respond

☐ Assess what emergency and/or personal items you have onboard that may be used to warm the victim

☐ Assess your ability to help the victim:

- Do you have warm, dry items to cover and wrap the person?
- Will you be able to get the victim to shore quickly?

☐ Exhibit a distress signal indicating your need for assistance if necessary

UNLOCK INTERACTIVE CONTENT

Scan this page

Learn how to safeguard your family against Cold Water Shock.

RESCUE PROCEDURE

STEP 1

Remove the person from the source of cold exposure (you should use the overboard rescue techniques, previously described in order, to remove the person from the water).

STEP 2

Dry the victim from head to toe and dress with layers of clothing. Provide dry shelter below deck if possible.

STEP 3

Attempt to slowly increase the victim's core body temperature by one or a combination of the following actions:

☐ Cover the victim's head and neck

☐ Wrap the victim in dry blankets or towels

☐ Cover the victim with an insulating device (such as a reflective heat blanket) and moisture barrier

REMEMBER:

- If the victim asks for a warm liquid, you may provide it to him/her—never give the victim alcohol or hot stimulants

- **Do not rub** and/or massage the victim's body or extremities in an attempt to warm them up—doing this may damage nerve endings at the skin and encourage cold blood from the extremities to move to the core of the body

- You can use your own body to transfer heat to the victim

- You should always carry a safety kit including equipment suitable for cold water and cold weather emergencies

SURVIVING COLD WATER

If you find yourself in cold water, do the following to increase your survival time:

IMMEDIATE ACTION

STEP 1

Assess the situation:

☐ **Is everyone wearing a PFD or life jacket?**
☐ **Can you get to shore or safety?**
☐ **Are there any boaters who can assist you?**
☐ **Are you able to signal or call for help?**

STEP 2

If you are within 50 m of shore and are able to swim to safety you should do so.

STEP 3

If you are injured, there is help close by, or you are further than 50 m from shore, you should stay where you are.

STEP 4

If you are alone and close to a floating object, you should climb onto the object to remove yourself from the cold water and save energy. However, you should only do so if you are able to get most of your body out of and above the water.

STEP 5

Immediately signal or call for help if you are able to do so.

HUDDLE POSITION

If you and your passengers find yourself exposed to cold water, and are unable to swim to shore or climb onto a floating object, you should assume the huddle position to increase your survival time:

- Place your arms around each other's mid to lower back and pull together so your chests are close to each other's sides
- Intertwine your legs
- Place any children in the middle of the huddle
- Keep unnecessary movements to a minimum in order to conserve energy

HEAT ESCAPE LESSENING POSITION (H.E.L.P.)

If you find yourself alone and exposed to cold water, use the **Heat Escape Lessening Position** (H.E.L.P.) to reduce heat loss from your core body temperature and delay the effects of hypothermia.

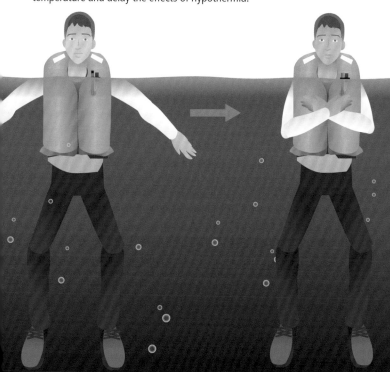

H.E.L.P IS PERFORMED AS FOLLOWS:

- Cross your arms tightly against your chest.
- Draw your knees up and against your chest.
- Keep your head and face out of the water.

BREAKDOWN AND MECHANICAL FAILURE

You are required by law to maintain your craft and safety equipment in proper working order. By regularly maintaining and inspecting your vessel, you'll reduce the risk of an unexpected breakdown.

If your craft has broken down or is inoperable due to mechanical failure:

STEP 1

Use an anchor to secure your craft, if necessary. If you are in a high traffic area, use a manual propelling device (such as a paddle or oars) to manoeuver your craft to a safe area before anchoring. If you have lost all power and are drifting towards significant danger, set your anchor immediately.

STEP 2

Investigate the cause of the breakdown or failure.

STEP 3

If possible, correct the problem.

STEP 4

If necessary, signal your need for assistance using a recognized distress signal.

REMEMBER:

You should always carry a tool kit including:

- Spare bulbs (appropriate for your craft)
- Spare fuses
- Grease, penetrating oil and rags
- Spare oil (4-Stroke or 2-Stroke depending on your type of engine)
- Spare safety lanyard (PWC operators)
- Spare spark plugs (appropriate for your engine)
- Basic toolset
- Common nuts and bolts
- Tie straps and duct tape

CARBON MONOXIDE

Carbon Monoxide (CO) is a deadly gas you can't see, smell or taste. CO is produced by anything that burns carbon-based fuel (gasoline, propane, charcoal, oil, etc.), including engines, generators, cooking ranges and heaters. CO spreads evenly throughout an enclosed space and is undetectable. Be aware when swimming from a boat equipped with pontoons. CO build-up can occur between the pontoons of a houseboat or a pontoon boat.

CO is inhaled into your lungs, cuts off the oxygen supply to your body and can kill in minutes. Be alert to flu-like symptoms which can include headaches, nausea and fatigue.

Operators of boats with fuel burning appliances, such as cooking ranges in houseboats, should be aware of the increased risks of CO poisoning. Swimmers or people being towed closely behind a boat with engines operating are also at increased risk of CO poisoning.

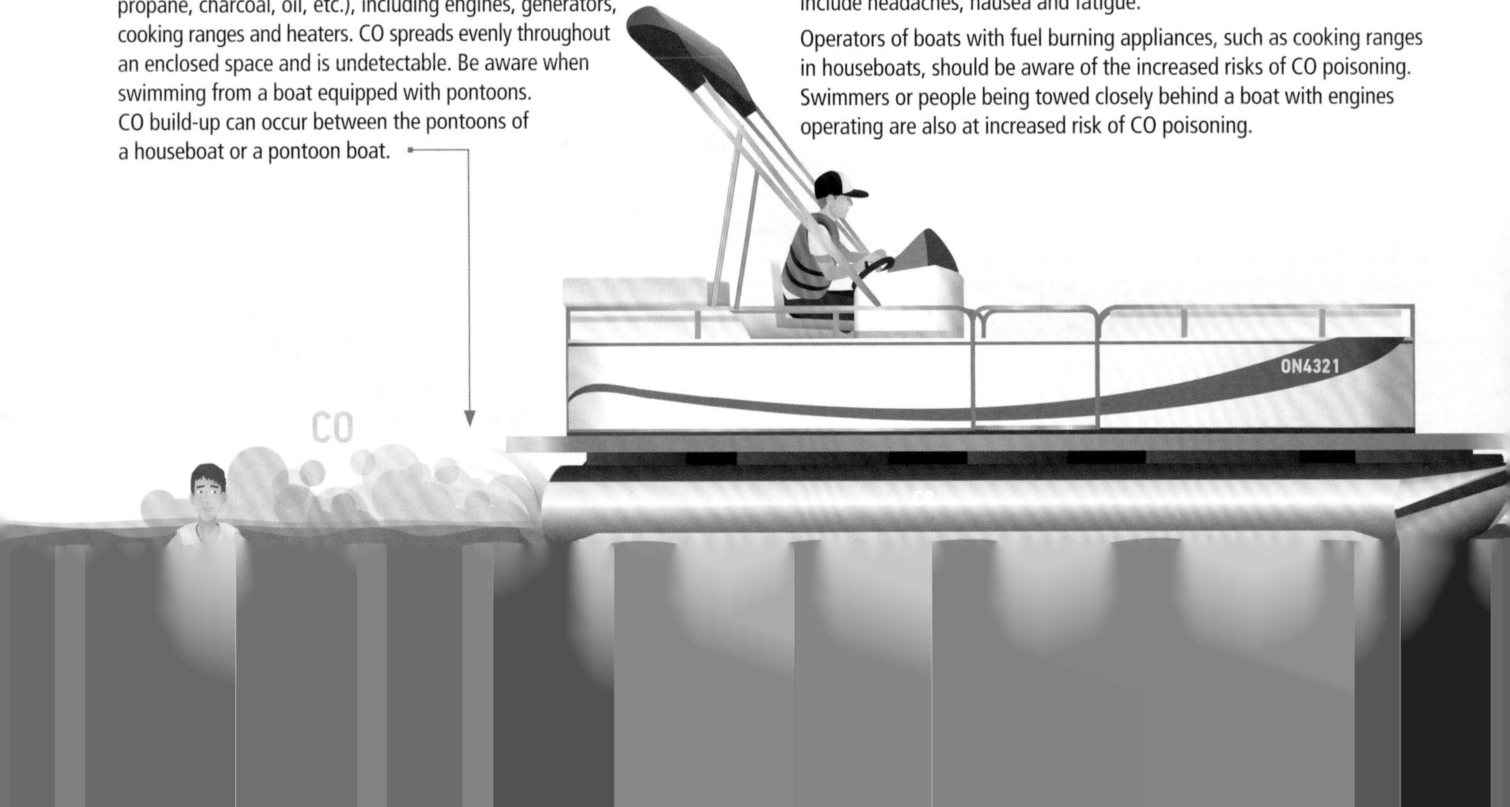

CO

ON4321

PROTECT YOURSELF FROM CO POISONING

Be sure to protect yourself and others from CO poisoning:

- Use a marine grade CO detector and check the batteries before each trip
- Only idle your engine in well-ventilated areas and recognize that winds from the stern can carry CO back onboard
- Only heat your boat's cabin or cook when in a well-ventilated area
- Use only fuel-burning engines or appliances that are certified or designed for marine use
- Proper use of ventilation systems and blowers on your craft can reduce the risk of CO poisoning

TREATING CO POISONING

- Move to fresh air away from the source of CO
- Seek medical/emergency help immediately

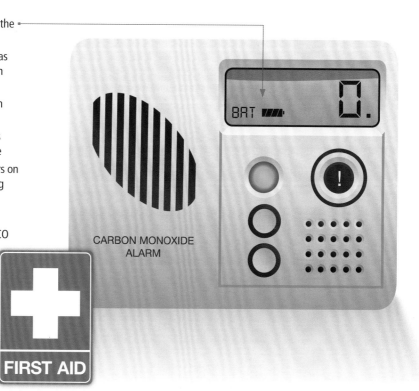

CARBON MONOXIDE
ALARM

FIRST AID

FIGHTING A FIRE

Boat fires can be caused by a number of factors including engine malfunctions, a fire in the galley or insufficient ventilation of an enclosed engine compartment. If a fire or explosion occurs, you can lessen the severity of the emergency by:

- Ensuring you have the mandatory fire-fighting equipment onboard
- Ensuring fire-fighting equipment is maintained regularly, in good working order and is readily accessible
- Ensuring you and your passengers respond with speed and effectiveness

HOW TO USE A FIRE EXTINGUISHER

Use the **P.A.S.S.** method to fight a fire on your boat:

- **P**ull the safety pin on the handle of the fire extinguisher

- **A**im at the base of the flames

SQUEEZE

- **S**queeze the handle

SWEEP

- **S**weep the fire by spraying from left to right in a sweeping motion

IMPORTANT FIRE EXTINGUISHER TIPS

Always remember to:

- Use an extinguisher designed for marine use
- Use an extinguisher with an external gauge (that indicates the condition of the charge)
- Remember that the extinguisher should be **turned upside down and shaken at least once per month to prevent the agent from clumping**
- C02 type extinguishers should be weighed annually and re-filled when they have diminished to 90% capacity
- Be aware that CO2 and Halon type extinguishers utilize colourless, odorless gases that displace oxygen (proceed with caution if using or storing these type of extinguishers in an enclosed area)
- Always use a fire extinguisher to put out electrical (Class C) or flammable liquid (Class B) fires—never use water as it will spread flammable liquid fires and will conduct electricity

SAFE BOATING TIP

Ensure the extinguisher is suitable for the type of fire you are trying to put out. Stand at a safe distance from the source of the flame (at least 1 meter back).

A   B   C

MAINTENANCE

A dead fire extinguisher is useless. Monthly inspections are required to keep fire extinguishers in proper working order. When inspecting a fire extinguisher, you should:

- Check the gauge to ensure the fire extinguisher is fully charged
- Look at the seals and hoses (if so equipped) and replace any that are cracked or broken
- Weigh extinguishers to make sure they meet the minimum weight levels stated on the label and recharge them if they contain less than 90% of their rated capacity

USING FUEL–BURNING APPLIANCES

Gas fumes, leaking propane and butane are heavier than air and will flow into the lower portions of your boat. These fumes are hard to remove and are highly explosive.

Be sure to follow these safety procedures when using butane and propane:

- Use fuel-burning appliances only in well-ventilated areas
- Secure gas cylinders, portable appliances and heaters so that unexpected movement doesn't cause a leak
- Always attend to open-flame heating, cooking or refrigeration systems
- Install fuel burning equipment according to manufacturer's instructions

UNDERSTANDING AND USING DISTRESS SIGNALS

Pleasure craft operators must be able to recognize, use and properly exhibit distress signals as required by the *Small Vessel Regulations.*

Depending on the size of your craft, and whether you are operating a power or sail-driven vessel, you are required to carry certain types of distress signals.

REMEMBER:
It is an offence to make or report a fake distress signal. Sending false distress signals takes time away from Search and Rescue Organizations, making them unavailable or farther away from real emergencies.

You are required to render assistance to any person, vessel or aircraft that signals distress. You are also required to offer assistance if you respond to a distress call and are asked by the vessel in distress to render assistance. If it is unreasonable (unsafe) to offer assistance, you are not required to help.

HAND SIGNAL

You can use your hands to signal distress: slowly raise and lower outstretched arms from above your head to each side of your body in repetition.

PORTABLE HORN / WHISTLE

You can use a portable horn or whistle to signal distress by continuously sounding it in one minute intervals. You can also signal S.O.S. by sounding three short blasts, then three long blasts, followed by three short blasts.

OTHER SOUND SIGNALLING DEVICES

You can signal distress by continuously sounding a fog-signaling device. You may also use a gunshot or other explosive sound-emitting device fired at one minute intervals.

WATERTIGHT FLASHLIGHT

A watertight flashlight can serve as an effective distress signal at night or during periods of reduced visibility. To signal distress with a flashlight, flash S.O.S. - three short flashes, then three long flashes, followed by three short flashes.

FLARES

There are 4 types of flares approved for use in Canada: **Types A, B, C and D**.

TYPE A
PARACHUTE FLARE

TYPE B
MULTI-STAR ROCKET

TYPE C
HAND-HELD FLARE

TYPE A PARACHUTE FLARE:

To discharge this aerial flare, read the manufacturer's instructions, hold away from your body, and pull the release mechanism. When launched, this red light flare reaches a height of approximately 300 m and burns for at least 40 seconds. This type of flare can be seen from water, land and air.

TYPE B MULTI-STAR ROCKET:

Also an aerial flare, this device fires two red stars to a height of approximately 100 m.

To discharge: Read the manufacturer's instructions and trigger the flare from a hand-held position. This type of flare will burn for four to five seconds and be visible from water, land and air.

TYPE C HAND-HELD FLARE:

This type of flare is designed for hand-held use and is not highly visible from a distance. Because of its limited visibility, this flare is most effective when used to help rescuers pin-point your location once they are near by.

To discharge: Read the manufacturer's instructions, hold downwind and away from your body and trigger the flare. This flare will burn intensely for at least one minute.

TYPE D BUOYANT OR HAND-HELD SMOKE FLARE:

This type of flare is most effective for daytime use. Hand-held or floating type smoke flares will discharge intense orange smoke for at least three minutes.

To discharge: Read the manufacturer's instructions, pull the release mechanism and hold the flare upright or toss it into the water.

REMEMBER:

- **A parachute flare works best during nighttime** (reaches a height of 300m and burns for 40 seconds!)
- Read the manufacturer's directions before using a flare or pyrotechnic device
- Flares must be approved for use by Transport Canada
- It is illegal to test or discharge a flare if not used for an emergency situation
- Only dispose of outdated flares in an approved manner—contact your local law enforcement agency, fire department, marine retailer or the Canadian Coast Guard for disposal procedures
- Check the date of manufacture and/or expiry date before using a flare
- Flares are valid for only four years from their date of manufacture

TYPE D
BUOYANT SMOKE FLARE

MARINE RADIO

You can use a maritime VHF radio to signal distress:

- Use maritime **VHF Channel 16** and repeat 'Pan Pan' three times to signal the need for assistance
- Use **VHF Channel 16** and repeat 'Mayday' three times to signal imminent danger and/or a life-threatening situation
- Once the appropriate distress signal is given, relay the following information:
  - The name of your vessel
  - Your position
  - The nature of the emergency
  - The type of assistance needed

If you are buying a new maritime VHF radio, be sure it has the new Digital Selective Calling (DSC) feature on channel 70. This feature provides automatic digital distress alerts. The Canadian Coast Guard provides DSC channel 70 service on the east and west coasts, as well as on the Great Lakes and St. Lawrence River.

SAFE BOATING TIP

If you have a cell phone onboard, call 911 to report your emergency. You can also call *16 to reach Canadian Coast Guard Marine Communications centres.

Keep in mind: making a cell phone call does not alert other boats on the water that you need help—and those boats could be the ones that help you first.

Remember, maritime VHF radio channel 16 is used for emergency purposes only. Once you contact another vessel on channel 16, you should switch to another working frequency.

MCTS centres provide Vessel Traffic Services (VTS) which alert boaters to intended movements of larger vessels in certain areas. MCTS centres also continuously broadcast Notices to Shipping and weather and ice reports on marine radio frequencies. Boaters should also be aware that the Canadian Coast Guard and MCTS centres will issue Safety Calls via marine radio to mariners, transmitting navigational safety notices and meteorological warnings.

LIMITATIONS OF CELL PHONES

While you can obtain search and rescue assistance from the nearest Canadian Coast Guard Marine Communications and Traffic Services (MCTS) centre by dialing *16 or #16 on a cell phone, a cell phone is not a good substitute for a marine radio. A maritime VHF radio is the best way of sending a distress alert because it alerts other boaters of the emergency at the same time and if nearby, they may be able to render assistance first.

- Cell phones can lose reception or get wet and damaged
- Calling from your cell phone does not alert nearby vessels that you are in distress
- Some cell signals cannot be traced back to your location by rescuers
- Not all cell providers offer the *16 and #16 service

You must obtain a maritime VHF/Restricted Operations Certificate (ROC) to use a maritime VHF radio for any reason in Canada. Courses and exams are administered by the Canadian Power & Sail Squadrons.

CODE FLAGS

Code flags can be used to signal distress. Use either of the following:

- The International Signal for Distress:
  Code flag 'N' (November) flown above Code Flag 'C' (Charlie)

- An orange distress cloth (or flag), displaying a black square and a black circle, identifiable from the air

OTHER DISTRESS SIGNALS

- **A dye marker** will colour the water around your vessel signalling your need for assistance
- **EPIRB:** an Emergency Position Indicating Response Beacon (EPIRB) sends a distress signal via satellite to a monitoring centre (EPIRBs must be registered with the National Beacon Registry at 1-800-727-9414)
- A high intensity white light flashing 50 to 70 times per minute
- A square shape (or arrangement of items resembling a square shape) positioned on your vessel, or in the water near your vessel
- Controlled flames showing onboard a vessel can also be used to signal distress. During daylight hours, choose a safe flammable substance (such as engine oil in a metal pan) to signal distress (always use caution when using an open flame onboard your craft)

MODULE 7 SUMMARY

Responding effectively in an emergency means that you need to be prepared with the right equipment and the right knowledge. You should know what to do if your craft capsizes, sinks or is swamped by high waves. Always carry the right equipment so that you can respond to hull leaks or flooding of your craft.

Be sure that you understand the correct techniques for rescuing a person overboard or a victim of hypothermia. People suffering from hypothermia exhibit progressive symptoms—you should be able to assess these symptoms and treat the victim accordingly. You should always be sure to carry appropriate cold water and cold weather survival gear when operating in harsh environments.

Always have onboard the required distress equipment for your size and type of craft. You should be able to choose an appropriate distress signal according to the circumstances, and be able to use it correctly to signal your need for help. You should also be able to recognize and respond to distress signals from other craft.

REMEMBER:
You may never be able to predict an emergency, but you can prepare for one.

MODULE 7 QUIZ

1   IF YOUR CRAFT HAS CAPSIZED, WHAT IS THE FIRST THING YOU SHOULD DO?

A   Swim for shore
B   Ensure that everyone is wearing a PFD or life jacket
C   Try to gather up any belongings that were thrown from the vessel
D   Attempt to signal to other boaters or to shore for help

2   WHAT DOES IT MEAN WHEN A PLEASURE CRAFT OPERATOR DISPLAYS A SQUARE FLAG WITH A BALL ABOVE OR BELOW IT?

A   The operator needs assistance
B   The operator has a diver down
C   The vessel is at anchor
D   The vessel is performing search and rescue operations

3   WHAT IS THE FIRST THING YOU SHOULD DO IF YOU ARE INVOLVED IN A COLLISION?

A   Exchange insurance information
B   Call the Coast Guard
C   Visually and verbally confirm everyone is accounted for and wearing a PFD or life jacket
D   Unless the damage is over $1000 you are not required to stop

4   WHICH OF THE FOLLOWING FLARES IS BEST SUITED TO NIGHTTIME USE?

A   Smoke Flare – Type D
B   Parachute Flare – Type A
C   Gun Flare – Type L
D   Dye Marker – Type F

MODULE 7 QUIZ

5   WHAT ARE THE SIGNS THAT A PERSON IS IN THE SECOND STAGE OF HYPOTHERMIA?

A   A slow and weak pulse, slow respiration and lack of co-ordination
B   A weak, irregular or absent pulse or respiration
C   Shivering and slurred speech
D   Loss of consciousness

6   WHEN IS IT LEGAL TO TEST A FLARE?

A   When you a purchase a new type of flare
B   When your flares have expired
C   When you are practising emergency procedures
D   It is illegal to test a flare

7   WHAT DOES IT MEAN IF A PLEASURE CRAFT OPERATOR REPEATS 'MAYDAY' USING A MARINE RADIO?

A   The operator is signalling the need for assistance
B   The operator is signalling imminent danger or a life threatening situation
C   The operator is signalling that he or she is returning to harbour
D   The operator is signalling that he or she has run out of fuel

8   YOU ARE THROWN FROM YOUR CRAFT INTO ROUGH, COLD SEAS. THE SUN IS GOING DOWN AND THE TEMPERATURE IS DROPPING. IN ORDER TO PRESERVE BODY HEAT, YOU SHOULD DO WHICH OF THE FOLLOWING?

A   Begin swimming or treading water
B   Assume the H.E.L.P position by crossing your arms tightly against your chest and drawing your knees up and against your body
C   Lie in the water face up
D   Assume the H.E.L.P position by waving your arms above your body

9)   YOU ARE OPERATING AN OPEN FISHING VESSEL IN ROUGH WATER CONDITIONS. SUDDENLY ONE OF YOUR PASSENGERS FALLS OVERBOARD. WHAT IS THE FIRST ACTION YOU SHOULD TAKE?

A   Immediately throw a life jacket or PFD to the victim and assign another passenger to keep watch of the person overboard
B   Immediately signal your need for assistance with an appropriate distress signal
C   Have a passenger take control of the boat so you may jump into the water to assist the victim
D   Throw the victim a reaching assist and pull them towards the vessel with the reaching assist

10   WHILE BOATING IN UNFAMILIAR WATERS, YOU HIT A SUBMERGED ROCK AND YOUR CRAFT BEGINS TAKING ON WATER. WHAT IS THE FIRST ACTION YOU SHOULD TAKE?

A   Speed up and quickly return to shore
B   Determine whether the passengers and the vessel are in danger
C   Stop the boat and use the horn to signal for assistance
D   Jump overboard and return to shore

1   WHAT IS THE PURPOSE OF A CONTROL BUOY?

A   Provides information of interest to boaters
B   Indicates speed limits to boaters
C   Marks an area where boating is prohibited
D   Marks an area where boating is restricted

2   WHICH OF THE FOLLOWING GOVERNS NAVIGATION RULES ON CANADIAN WATERWAYS?

A   The *Small Vessel Regulations*
B   The *Collision Regulations*
C   The *Charts and Nautical Publications Regulation*s
D   The *Contraventions Act*

3   WHICH OF THE FOLLOWING IS THE CORRECT DEFINITION FOR THE 'PORT' SIDE OF A BOAT?

A   To the left side of your vessel when looking forward
B   To the right side of your vessel when looking forward
C   The front of the vessel
D   The rear of the vessel

4   WHY DO BOATS WITH GREATER THAN 0.5 M FREEBOARD REQUIRE AN APPROVED RE-BOARDING DEVICE?

A   To allow easy re-boarding from the water
B   To assist with boarding your vessel at a dock
C   To assist with loading equipment
D   To assist when refueling

5   WHICH ACT, CODE OR REGULATION REQUIRES THAT SAFETY EQUIPMENT BE CARRIED ONBOARD AT ALL TIMES?

A   The *Criminal Code of Canada*
B   The *Small Vessel Regulations*
C   The *Boating Restriction Regulations*
D   The *Collision Regulations*

6   UNDER WHAT CONDITIONS MIGHT A MAGNETIC COMPASS BE NEGATIVELY AFFECTED AND PROVIDE YOU WITH INCORRECT INFORMATION?

A   When the compass is on the inside of a boat cabin
B   When the compass is exposed to sunlight
C   When in the proximity of metallic and electrical devices
D   When held higher than 4 ft above the boat

7   YOU SHOULD ALWAYS ENSURE WHICH OF THE FOLLOWING WHEN ANCHORING YOUR CRAFT?

A   Ensure the inboard end of the anchor line is securely attached to the anchor
B   Ensure the outboard end of the anchor line is securely attached to the craft
C   Ensure the inboard end of the anchor line is securely attached to the craft
D   Ensure the anchor line is 10 times the length of your craft

8   DO BOATS INVOLVED IN FISHING ACTIVITIES, SUCH AS THOSE TRAWLING WITH NETS, HAVE RIGHT-OF-WAY OVER NON-POWERED CRAFT?

A   Yes
B   No
C   Only in large bodies of water
D   Only at night

9 WHICH COMMON BOATING BEHAVIOUR IS A FACTOR IN APPROXIMATELY 40% OF CANADA'S BOATING-RELATED FATALITIES?

A Speeding in the boat
B Collisions with local hazards
C Consuming alcohol or drugs
D Overloading the boat

10 THE SMALL VESSEL REGULATIONS REQUIRE THAT CERTAIN PLEASURE CRAFT MUST BE LICENSED, UNLESS THEY ARE REGISTERED. WHICH ARE THEY?

A All craft over 6 m in length
B All craft regardless of their size and length
C All craft that are able to transport passengers
D All craft powered by 10 hp (7.5 KW) or more

11 WHEN SHOULD YOU DETERMINE THE LOCAL WEATHER FORECAST?

A Immediately after you head out
B Before you head out
C As long as its not storming, you don't need to worry
D 7 days prior to your departure

12 WHEN MUST A SPOTTER BE PRESENT WHEN TOWING A PERSON WATER-SKIING, WAKEBOARDING OR USING ANY OTHER TOWABLE DEVICE?

A A spotter must always be present
B Only when using a PWC
C When the passenger being towed is under 16
D Only when towing at night

13 WHICH TYPE OF MOTORIZED VESSEL REQUIRES YOU TO CARRY PROOF OF COMPETENCY, SUCH AS A PLEASURE CRAFT OPERATOR CARD, ONBOARD AT ALL TIMES, WHEN OPERATING?

A All pleasure craft propelled (or designed to be propelled) by a motor
B Personal watercrafts (PWCs)
C Sailboats propelled by a motor
D All vessels over 10 tons

14 WHICH LAW REQUIRES THAT YOU MAINTAIN YOUR BOAT AND EQUIPMENT IN SEAWORTHY CONDITION?

A The *Boating Restriction Regulations*
B The *Maintenance Regulations*
C The *Criminal Code of Canada*
D The *Contraventions Act*

15 WHAT ACTIONS SHOULD YOU TAKE IF OVERTAKING ANOTHER POWER-DRIVEN VESSEL?

A You are the give-way craft and if possible pass on the starboard side
B You are the give-way craft and if possible pass on the port side
C You have the right of way and can pass on either side you want
D You should not pass and just wait until they change direction

16 HOW LONG SHOULD YOU OPERATE THE ENGINE VENTILATION SYSTEM ('BLOWER') BEFORE STARTING THE ENGINE?

A At least 2 minutes
B At least 6 minutes
C At least 4 minutes
D It is not always necessary

17 WHEN MUST A LIFE JACKET OR PERSONAL FLOTATION DEVICE BE REPLACED?

A   If it is ripped or in poor condition
B   Once the expiraton date on the label has passed
C   They must be replaced every 5 years
D   They must be replaced every 6 years

18 WHAT IS THE MOST ENVIRONMENTALLY-FRIENDLY WAY TO RE-FUEL A PORTABLE GAS TANK?

A   Use gas pumps that are designated for marine use only
B   Use an extra container to fill the portable tank
C   Disembark the boat and bring the portable tank to shore for re-fuelling
D   Operate the 'blower' while you are re-fueling to remove fumes

19 WHICH OF THE FOLLOWING IS THE CORRECT DEFINITION OF A 'PLEASURE CRAFT'?

A   Any vessel, ship, boat or other type of craft that is used exclusively for pleasure or recreation
B   Any vessel, ship, boat or other type of craft
C   Any vessel, ship, boat or other type of craft that is primarily used for pleasure or recreation
D   Any vessel, ship, boat or other type of craft that can carry passengers

20 WHAT TYPE OF HULL IS DESIGNED TO CUT THROUGH THE WATER RATHER THAN GLIDING ON TOP OF IT?

A   Displacement hull
B   Planing hull
C   Pontoon hull
D   Round-bottom hull

21 ARE PLEASURE CRAFT LEGALLY REQUIRED TO BE FITTED WITH A NOISE MUFFLING DEVICE (SUCH AS A MUFFLER)?

A   Pleasure craft are not required to be fitted with a noise muffling device
B   A noise muffling device is only required when using your boat within 9.26 km (5 nautical miles) of a Provincial Park
C   Only boats larger than 20 m are required to have a noise muffling device
D   Pleasure craft are not permitted within 9.26 km (5 nautical miles) from any shore unless they are fitted with a noise muffling device

22 WHAT ACTION SHOULD YOU TAKE IF YOU SEE A SERIES OF WHITE BUOYS?

A   Speed up and leave the designated area
B   Steer well clear as the buoy is marking an underwater hazard
C   Steer well clear as the buoys are marking a swimming area
D   You are approaching a restricted mooring area

23 IF YOUR CRAFT HAS CAPSIZED, WHAT IS THE FIRST THING YOU SHOULD DO?

A   Swim for shore
B   Ensure that everyone is wearing a PFD or life jacket
C   Try to gather up any belongings that were thrown from the vessel
D   Attempt to signal to other boaters or to shore for help

24 WHAT IS THE PURPOSE OF A BIFURCATION BUOY?

A   Identifies an isolated danger
B   Marks a head dam or obstruction
C   Marks the junction of two or more channels
D   Used to signal a 'diver-down'

25 WHAT DOES THE MAXIMUM LOAD ON A COMPLIANCE NOTICE REFER TO?

A The weight of persons, gear, equipment, supplies, fuel and motor assembly
B The weight of gear and fuel–not including the weight of passengers
C The weight of the boat during rainy operating conditions
D The weight of the passengers, gear and equipment, not including the motor

26 WHAT IS THE BEST WAY TO ENSURE YOU HAVE ENOUGH FUEL ONBOARD?

A Rule of thirds - 1/3 out, 1/3 back and 1/3 in reserve
B Rule of halves - 1/2 out and back, 1/2 reserve
C You should always fill your tank before departing
D Calculate your gas mileage based on 5 nautical miles per gallon

27 YOU ARE THROWN FROM YOUR CRAFT INTO ROUGH, COLD SEAS. THE SUN IS GOING DOWN AND THE TEMPERATURE IS DROPPING. IN ORDER TO PRESERVE BODY HEAT, YOU SHOULD DO WHICH OF THE FOLLOWING?

A Begin swimming or treading water
B Assume the H.E.L.P position by crossing your arms against your chest and drawing your knees up and against your body
C Lie in the water face up to keep your body as much out of the water as possible
D Assume the H.E.L.P position by waving your arms above your body

28 WHICH THREE COLOURS ARE USED FOR NAVIGATION LIGHTS?

A Red, green and blue
B Red, green and yellow
C Green, red and white
D White, blue and yellow

29 WHAT ARE THE SIGNS THAT A PERSON IS IN THE SECOND STAGE OF HYPOTHERMIA?

A A slow and weak pulse, slow respiration and lack of co-ordination
B A weak, irregular or absent pulse or respiration
C Shivering and slurred speech
D Loss of consciousness

30 WHAT IS THE FRONT OF A BOAT CALLED?

A Beam
B Bow
C Gunwale
D Bilge

31 THE CHARTS AND NAUTICAL PUBLICATIONS REGULATIONS REQUIRE WHICH OF THE FOLLOWING?

A That boaters are required to carry marine charts under all circumstances
B That marine charts depict marina service locations
C That boaters must carry the largest scale charts for the area in which they are navigating
D That if your boat is equipped with a marine GPS you are still required by law to have printed charts

32 WHILE BOATING IN UNFAMILIAR WATERS, YOU HIT A SUBMERGED ROCK AND YOUR CRAFT BEGINS TAKING ON WATER. WHAT IS THE FIRST ACTION YOU SHOULD TAKE?

A Speed up and quickly return to shore
B Determine whether the passengers and the vessel are in danger
C Stop the boat and use the horn to signal for assistance
D Jump overboard and return to shore

33 YOU SEE A BUOY THAT IS WHITE IN COLOUR WITH TWO HORIZONTAL ORANGE BANDS AND AN ORANGE DIAMOND. WHAT TYPE OF BUOY ARE YOU APPROACHING?

A   Cautionary Buoy
B   Anchorage Buoy
C   Control Buoy
D   Hazard Buoy

34 UNDER WHICH OF THE FOLLOWING CONDITIONS ARE YOU REQUIRED TO HELP OTHER BOATERS IN DISTRESS?

A   Only when it safe for you to do so and it doesn't put yourself and/or your passengers at risk
B   You are always required to help other boaters in distress
C   Only if your boat is equipped with a VHF radio
D   Only if you have an EPIRB distress beacon onboard

35 WHICH OF THE FOLLOWING IS THE CORRECT DEFINITION OF A BOAT'S HULL?

A   The portion of the pleasure craft in the water
B   The portion of the pleasure craft both in and above the water
C   The body of the pleasure craft excluding masts, sails, rigging, equipment or machinery
D   The body of the pleasure craft excluding machinery

36 WHAT COLOUR IS A SWIMMING BUOY?

A   White
B   Red
C   Orange
D   Blue

37 WHAT IS THE FIRST THING YOU SHOULD DO IF YOU ARE INVOLVED IN A COLLISION?

A   Exchange insurance information
B   Call the Coast Guard
C   Visually and verbally confirm everyone is accounted for and wearing a PFD or life jacket
D   Unless the damage is over $1000 you are not required to stop

38 HOW MANY CANADIAN-APPROVED LIFE JACKETS OR PFDS ARE YOU REQUIRED TO CARRY ONBOARD YOUR BOAT?

A   At least one SOLAS type life jacket
B   Two SOLAS types and two regular types
C   One for every person onboard the boat
D   One for every seat on the boat

39 WHAT IS THE PURPOSE OF DE-ACTIVATING A TRIP PLAN (SAIL PLAN) UPON YOUR RETURN FROM A BOATING TRIP?

A   To alert commercial traffic that the waterway is now clear for use
B   To make sure search and rescue teams do not go looking for you
C   To meet the *Operation Regulation* requirement to de-activate a sail plan
D   To keep a map of the route in case the operator decides to repeat it

40 YOU ARE APPROACHING ANOTHER CRAFT AFTER SUNSET AND SEE A GREEN AND WHITE LIGHT. WHAT ACTION SHOULD YOU TAKE?

A   The other craft is approaching from your port side—use caution and maintain your speed and direction
B   Immediately alter your course and pass in front of the other craft
C   Immediately alter your course and pass behind the other craft
D   The other craft is approaching from your starboard side—alter your course

41 WHAT IS THE PENALTY FOR A PERSON WHO KNOWINGLY OPERATES A BOAT IN UNSEAWORTHY CONDITION?

A Charges will be laid under the *Criminal Code*
B Their Captain's Certificate will be suspended
C Their boat will be impounded for 60 days
D Charges will be laid under the *Collision Regulations*

42 WHY SHOULD YOU CONSIDER 'RIGHT OF SWING' WHEN ANCHORING YOUR CRAFT?

A Considering 'right of swing' will ensure you do not anchor in a navigational channel
B Considering 'right of swing' will ensure you do not anchor in a shipping lane
C Considering 'right of swing' will ensure you leave enough room between you and other anchored craft
D 'Right of swing' ensures you display the proper anchor lights

43 WHAT IS THE STAND-ON CRAFT?

A The craft that has the right-of-way
B The craft that does not have the right-of-way
C A craft that is at anchor
D A craft that is slowing down

44 IF YOU APPROACH A JUNCTION DAY BEACON WHILE BOATING, WHAT IS THAT SIGN MARKING?

A A protected environmental zone where only boats 10 hp and under may enter
B A point where the channel divides and the preferred direction for boaters to take

C The intersection of a shipping lane and a commercial lane where boat traffic is limited
D The entrance to a military port area where boat operation is highly restricted

45 CARDINAL BUOYS ARE USED TO IDENTIFY WHICH OF THE FOLLOWING?

A Persons engaged in diving activities
B Safe water on the North, South, East or West side of the buoy
C Specific hazards such as submerged power lines
D A safe anchorage area

46 WHEN IS IT LEGAL TO TEST A FLARE?

A When you a purchase a new type of flare
B When your flares have expired
C When you are practising emergency procedures
D It is illegal to test a flare

47 WHICH OF THE FOLLOWING IS THE NUMBER ONE CAUSE OF BOATING-RELATED FATALITIES IN CANADA?

A Collision with another boat
B Capsizing emergencies
C Not wearing a life jacket or PFD
D Alcohol consumption

48 THE WATER DISPLACED BY THE MOVEMENT OF A BOAT IS CALLED?

A Wake
B Wash
C Tide
D Surf

49 WHEN ANCHORING FOR THE NIGHT WHAT LIGHT(S) SHOULD YOU DISPLAY?

A   Red and green sidelight
B   All-round white light
C   Red and green sidelights and all-round light
D   White stern light

50 YOU ARE OPERATING AN OPEN FISHING VESSEL IN ROUGH WATER CONDITIONS. SUDDENLY ONE OF YOUR PASSENGERS FALLS OVERBOARD. WHAT IS THE FIRST ACTION YOU SHOULD TAKE?

A   Immediately throw a life jacket or PFD to the victim and assign another passenger to keep watch of the person overboard
B   Immediately signal your need for assistance with an appropriate distress signal
C   Have a passenger take control of the boat so you may jump into the water to assist the victim
D   Throw the victim a reaching assist and pull them towards the vessel with the reaching assist

MODULE QUIZ ANSWER KEY

	MODULE 1		MODULE 2		MODULE 3
1	C	1	A	1	B
2	A	2	D	2	C
3	A	3	A	3	A
4	A	4	C	4	C
5	C	5	B	5	A
6	B	6	B	6	B
7	D	7	B	7	B
8	A	8	D	8	C
9	B	9	C	9	A
10	C	10	A	10	C

PRACTICE EXAM ANSWER KEY

MODULE 4		MODULE 5		MODULE 6		MODULE 7	
1	C	1	C	1	C	1	B
2	B	2	A	2	B	2	A
3	A	3	A	3	D	3	C
4	B	4	B	4	C	4	B
5	C	5	C	5	C	5	A
6	C	6	A	6	B	6	D
7	A	7	C	7	A	7	B
8	D	8	A	8	D	8	B
9	C	9	B	9	C	9	A
10	B	10	A	10	D	10	B

1	D	18	C	35	C
2	B	19	A	36	A
3	A	20	A	37	C
4	A	21	D	38	C
5	B	22	C	39	B
6	C	23	B	40	A
7	C	24	C	41	A
8	A	25	A	42	C
9	C	26	A	43	A
10	D	27	B	44	B
11	B	28	C	45	B
12	A	29	A	46	D
13	A	30	B	47	C
14	C	31	C	48	A
15	A	32	B	49	B
16	C	33	D	50	A
17	A	34	A		

GLOSSARY

ABAFT:
The direction towards the stern or near the back of the pleasure craft.

ABREAST:
Side by side; by the side of the craft.

ADRIFT:
Loose, not on moorings or towline.

AFT:
Towards the rear of the pleasure craft.

AGROUND:
Touching or fast to the waterway bottom.

AHEAD:
The direction in front of the bow of a pleasure craft.

AIDS TO NAVIGATION:
Markers on land and water which advise the boat operator of the direction of the best or preferred route.

ALL-ROUND LIGHT:
A light showing an unbroken light over an arc of the sky-line of 360°.

AMID SHIP:
In or toward the centre of the boat.

ANCHOR LINE:
A line used to hold a vessel fast to the anchor.

ANCHORAGE:
A suitable place for anchoring in relation to the wind, seas and bottom.

ASTERN:
Directly behind the back of the craft. The position pointing behind the pleasure craft.

BEAM:
The widest part of a craft measured from side to side.

BEARING:
The direction of an object (vessel, buoy, etc.) from an observer; bearings can be visual, by radio, or by radar.

BILGE:
The lowest point of a vessel's interior hull.

BLOWER:
A device that blows fuel vapors trapped inside the bilge to the outside.

BOAT:
A general term for a waterborne vehicle smaller than a ship. The terms pleasure craft, vessel, or powerboat may also be used.

BLUE FLASHING LIGHT:
Identifies a government operated vessel.

BOW:
The forward part of a pleasure craft.

BOW LINE:
A docking line leading from the bow to prevent the vessel from moving astern.

BOW LIGHTS:
Navigation lights located at the bow of the craft.

BUOY:
An anchored float used for marking a position on the water and identifying the best direction for a craft to travel.

BUOYANT HEAVING LINE:
A floating line not less than 15 m in length used to help an individual in distress.

CANOE:
A light, open, slender boat that has pointed ends and is propelled by paddles.

COMPLIANCE NOTICE:
A metal plate permanently mounted on a vessel by the manufacturer which describes the total weight limit allowed onboard, the total number of adults allowed onboard and the maximum horsepower rated for the craft.

CAPSIZE:
To turn over.

CAST OFF:
Undo mooring lines in preparation for departure.

CATAMARAN:
A twin-hulled boat, with hulls side by side.

CCG:
Canadian Coast Guard.

BOATsmart! | assure

INSURANCE FOR SMART BOATERS

BEST-IN-CLASS COVERAGE FOR LESS

GET A FREE ONLINE QUOTE TODAY >

BoatSmartAssure.com

1-855-829-6753

YOU CAN COUNT ON US. ALWAYS.

SAVE $10

ON ONLINE PURCHASES OF $50 OR MORE

BOATsmart! Marine Safety™ Products
work when you need them most.

BoatSmartMarine.com™

ONLINE DISCOUNT CODE BS 616

BOATsmart!
MARINE SAFETY

Quality · Innovation · Dependability

CHART:
A sea and/or in-land waterway map for use by mariners and operators to assist in navigation, identify hazards, traffic routes, navigation aids, anchorage areas, and adjacent coastal areas.

CHINE:
The intersection of the bottom and sides of a flat or V-bottomed boat.

CLEAT:
A fitting to which lines are tied.

COCKPIT:
An opening in the deck from which the boat is controlled.

COURSE:
The direction in which a boat is steered.

COMPASS:
A tool used to indicate direction and to aid the operator of a pleasure craft in finding bearing.

CURRENT:
The horizontal movement of the water in a specific direction.

DANGER ZONE:
The area encompassed from dead ahead of a vessel to just abaft the starboard beam.

DECK:
A permanent covering over a compartment or hull where you can walk or stand.

DISPLACEMENT:
The weight of water displaced by a floating vessel, thus, a boat's weight.

DISPLACEMENT HULL:
A type of hull that plows through the water.

DOCK:
A protected water area in which vessels are secured.

D.O.T.:
Department of Transport, Canada.

DOWNWIND:
A direction leeward, with the wind.

DRAFT:
The minimum depth of water in which a pleasure craft will float freely.

EBB:
A receding current.

FLARE:
A pyrotechnic signalling device used when a boater is in distress.

FLAME ARRESTOR:
A safety device to prevent explosion from engine exhaust backfire.

FENDERS:
Various devices used to cushion shocks and protect the sides of pleasure craft.

FREEBOARD:
The minimum vertical distance from the surface of the water to the gunwale.

FORE:
Towards the front of the craft.

GALLEY:
The kitchen area of a craft.

GALE WARNING:
Defined as winds with a sustained wind speed of 34 to 47 knots (63 to 87 km/h)

GIVE-WAY-VESSEL:
A term used to describe the vessel which must yield in meeting, crossing, or overtaking situations.

GLOBAL POSITIONING SYSTEM (GPS):
A form of position finding using radio transmissions from satellites.

GUNWALE:
The upper edge of each side of the hull of a craft.

HATCH:
An opening in a boat's deck fitted with a watertight cover.

HEADING:
The direction in which a vessel's bow points at any given time.

HEADWAY:
The forward motion of a boat.

H.E.L.P:
Heat Escape Lessoning Position.

HUDDLE POSITION:
The Huddle Position can help to preserve the body's core temperature and reduce the effects of hypothermia.

HULL:
The main body of a pleasure craft, excluding masts, sails, rigging, machinery and equipment.

HYPOTHERMIA:
A condition that occurs when there is a drop in core body temperature below normal levels.

INBOARD ENGINE:
A motor fitted inside a boat.

IMPELLER:
A blade (much like a propeller) that rotates inside a jet pump (housing), forcing water out a nozzle in order to move the craft.

KAYAK:
A long, narrow boat, pointed at both ends, made of a light frame that is powered with a double-bladed paddle.

KEEL:
The centerline or backbone of a vessel.

LEEWARD:
The direction away from the wind.

LIFE JACKET:
A life jacket is a personal flotation device that is designed to turn an unconscious person face-up in the water.

LIGHT WINDS:
Winds with a wind speed less than 12 knots (22 km/h)

LOAD:
The maximum weight a vessel can safely carry (including people, motor, fuel and equipment).

LOCK:
A structure having moveable gates for ships and boats to pass up and down different water levels in a canal, river, or tidal basin.

LOOKOUT:
Operators are required to maintain a constant lookout using every available means, to determine whether there is any risk of collision with another vessel.

MASTHEAD LIGHT:
A white light placed over the fore and aft center line of a pleasure craft.

MAYDAY:
A VHF or radiotelephone distress signal that is used when a craft and crew are in a hazardous or life-threatening situation.

MODERATE WINDS:
Moderate Winds are winds with a wind speed of 12 to 19 knots (22 to 35 km/h).

MOORING:
To fasten or secure a boat to a fixed point.

NAVIGATION:
Conducting a boat safely from one point to another.

NAVIGATION RULES:
The laws and regulations governing the movement of vessels in relation to each other, including right-of-way rules.

OPERATOR:
The person who is responsible for the operation of a pleasure craft.

OUTBOARD:
A detachable engine with a shaft and propeller mounted on a boat's transom.

OVERBOARD:
Over the side of the boat.

OVERTAKING:
When a vessel is passing another from behind.

'PAN, PAN':
A VHF radio or radiotelephone distress signal used to designate a non-life threatening emergency.

PERSONAL FLOTATION DEVICE (PFD):
A PFD is a device which, when worn properly, uses flotation to keep the wearer's chin above the water.

PERSONAL WATERCRAFT (PWC):
A pleasure craft with an enclosed hull, powered by an enclosed jet-propulsion system.

PLANING:
When a boat moves over the top of the water rather than through the water.

PLANING HULL:
A type of hull shaped to glide across the surface of the water when power is applied.

PLEASURE CRAFT:
A boat, a ship or vessel that is used exclusively for recreation.

PORT:
The left side of a pleasure craft looking forward.

POWER-DRIVEN VESSEL (POWERBOAT):
A pleasure craft that is propelled through the water by a motor.

PRE-DEPARTURE CHECKLIST:
A checklist that aids a pleasure craft operator in determining their preparedness for a trip on the water.

PROPELLER:
Blades attached to an engine shaft that rotate, forces water back and moves the craft forward.

REACHING ASSIST:
A device used to help you reach a person in distress.

RECOMMENDED GROSS LOAD CAPACITY:
Identifies the total weight that can be safely carried in the craft and includes the weight of persons, equipment, stores, fuel, motor and steering controls.

RIGGING:
The wire rope, rods, lines, hardware and other equipment that support and control the spars and sails of sailboats.

RIGHT-OF-WAY:
The right of a vessel to cross in front of other vessels.

RING BUOY (LIFE BUOY):
A circular buoy that is attached to a buoyant line of not less than 15 m in length.

ROWBOAT:
Small boat propelled by oars.

RUDDER:
A vertical plate or board affixed at the stern of a vessel for steering.

RUNNING LIGHTS:
Lights required to be shown on boats underway between sunset and sunrise and during periods of reduced visibility.

RODE:
A combination of rope and chain attached to an anchor.

SAILING VESSEL:
Any vessel powered by wind and sail, provided that propelling machinery, if fitted, is not being used.

SAFE SPEED:
An operation speed at which a vessel can proceed and be able to take proper and effective action to avoid a collision.

SEAWORTHY:
A boat or a boat's equipment meets the usual sea conditions.

SIDELIGHTS:
A green light on a boat's starboard side and a red light on a boat's port side.

SMALL CRAFT WARNING:
Sustained wind speeds in the range of 20 to 33 knots (37 to 61 km/h).

S.O.S.:
Internationally recognized distressed signal that can be sent by sound signal, light or radio (3 short blasts, 3 long blasts, and 3 short blasts).

STAND-ON-VESSEL:
The vessel which has right-of-way during a meeting, crossing, or overtaking situation.

STARBOARD:
The right side of a boat when looking forward.

STERN:
The back part of a boat.

STERN LIGHT:
A white light placed as near as possible to the stern of a vessel.

STORM WARNING:
Sustained wind speeds in the range of 48 to 63 knots (89 to 117 km/h).

STRONG WINDS:
Winds with sustained wind speeds in the range of 20 to 33 knots (37 to 61 km/h).

SWAMP:
To fill with water, but not settle to the bottom.

THROTTLE:
A mechanism used to regulate the flow of fuel, and thus the speed, of an internal combustion engine.

TIDE:
The periodic rise and fall of water level in the oceans. Occurs every 12 hours and is caused by the gravitational pull of the moon.

TOPOGRAPHICAL MAP:
A map depicting natural and artificial features of the land area including elevation contours, shoreline rocks, land features above the water, and cultural features.

TRANSOM:
The stern cross-section of the back of the boat.

TRIM:
The fore and aft balance of the craft and its horizontal position in the water.

TRIP PLAN:
A document that describes both your vessel and your travel plans on the water.

UNDERWAY:
A vessel that is in motion.

VESSEL:
Every description of a water craft, capable of being used as a means of water transportion.

VESSEL LICENSE:
A Vessel license is a document that contains a set of ID numbers that must be displayed on your boat for identification purposes.

VHF RADIOTELEPHONE:
Very High Frequency radio.

WAKE:
The moving waves, track or path that a boat leaves behind it when moving across the water.

WASH:
The loose or broken water left behind in the trail of a pleasure craft, thrown aft by the propeller.

WINDWARD:
Toward the direction from which the wind is coming.

INDEX

RESOURCES

BOATING SAFETY INFO HEADQUARTERS

Transport Canada, Marine Safety

Office of Boating Safety (AMSRO)
Tower C, Place de Ville
330 Sparks Street
Ottawa, Ontario
K1A 0N8

Email: obs-bsn@tc.gc.ca
Phone: 1-800-267-6687
TTY/TDD: 1-888-675-6863

BOATING SAFETY INFO (REGIONAL)

Pacific Region (British Columbia)

700-800 Burrard Street
Vancouver, BC
V6Z 2J8

Email: obs-pac-bsn@tc.gc.ca
Phone: (604) 666-2681

Prairie & Northern Region (Alberta, Saskatchewan, Manitoba, Yukon, Northwest Territories & Nunavut)
344 Edmonton Street
P.O. Box 8550
Winnipeg, Manitoba
R3C 0P6

Email: obs-pnr-bsn@tc.gc.ca
Phone: 1-888-463-0521

Ontario Region

100 Front St, South
Sarnia, Ontario
N7T 2M4

Email: obs-ontario-bsn@tc.gc.ca
Phone:1-800-267-6687

Quebec Region

Transport Canada Centre
1550 Estimauville Avenue, 4th floor
Quebec, Quebec
G1J 0C8

Email: obs-quebec-bsn@tc.gc.ca
Phone: (418) 648-5331

Atlantic Region (New Brunswick, Prince Edward Island and Nova Scotia)

45 Alderney Drive, 11th Floor
P.O. Box 1013
Dartmouth, Nova Scotia
B2Y 4K2

Email: obs-atl-bsn@tc.gc.ca
Phone:1-855-859-3123

Newfoundland and Labrador

100 New Gower Street, 7th Floor
P.O. Box 1300
St. John's, NL
A1C 6H8

Email: obs-atl-bsn@tc.gc.ca
Phone: 1-800-230-3693

RESOURCES

SEARCH AND RESCUE

Pacific Coast

Joint Rescue Coordination Centre
Victoria, B.C.

Email: jrccvictoria@sarnet.dnd.ca
Phone: 1-800-567-5111
Cellular: #727
Satellite, local, or out of area:
250-413-8933

Great Lakes and Arctic

Joint Rescue Coordination Centre
CFB Trenton

24-hour emergency numbers:
Toll-free (Canada): 1-800-267-7270
Phone: (613) 965-3870

St. Lawrence River

Maritime Rescue Sub-Centre Quebec
Toll free (within region):
1-800-463-4393
Phone: 1-418-648-3599

Newfoundland & Labrador Coast

Maritime Rescue Sub-Centre
St. John's
Toll free (within region):
1-800-563-2444
Phone: 1-902-427-8200

Maritime Coast (Nova Scotia, New Brunswick, PEI)

Joint Rescue Coordination Centre
Halifax
Toll free (within region):
1-800-565-1582
Phone: 1-902-427-8200

MARINE POLLUTION REPORTING

Newfoundland and Labrador
1-800-563-9089 (24 hours)

Central and Arctic
1-800-265-0237 (24 hours)

Quebec
1-800-363-4735 (24 hours)

Maritimes
1-800-565-1633 (24 hours)

Pacific
1-800-889-8852 (24 hours)

CHARTS AND NAUTICAL PUBLICATIONS

Canadian Hydrographic Service
615 Booth Street
Ottawa ON K1A 0E6

Phone: (613) 998-4931
Toll-free: 1-866-546-3613

WEATHER FORECASTS

Channel 21B, 25B and 83B on the
Atlantic Coast and Great Lakes

Channel 21B, and Wx1, 2, 3
on the Pacific Coast

VHF broadcasts from Weatheradio
Canada (Environment Canada)
http://weatheroffice.ec.gc.ca/marine/
index_e.html

TIDE TABLES

Canadian tide and water level
information can be found on the
web at: http://www.tides.gc.ca/eng

HOW TO TIE BOATING KNOTS

It's a great idea to learn how to tie boating knots. Familiarize yourself with the knots below and use them to secure your boat properly.

REMEMBER:
Practice makes perfect! Practice your knots so that you're ready to use them when you need to!

THE BOWLINE:
Holds tight and comes apart easily.

 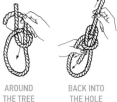

OUT OF THE HOLE	AROUND THE TREE	BACK INTO THE HOLE

THE REEF KNOT (A.K.A. SQUARE KNOT):
Ties two lines together.

THE CLOVE HITCH
Easily ties your boat temporarily to a piling.

THE HORN CLEAT HITCH
Keeps your boat securely tied.

AROUND UNDER	OVER AND UNDER	MAKE A LOOP	PULL IT SNUG

Alpha
Diver Down, Keep Clear

 Bravo
Dangerous Cargo

 Charlie
Yes

 Delta
Keep Clear

 Echo
Keep Clear

 Foxtrot
Disabled

 Golf
Want a pilot

 Hotel
Pilot Onboard

 India
Altering Course to Port

 Juliet
On Fire; Keep Clear

 Kilo
Desire to communicate

 Lima
Stop instantly

 Mike
I Am Stopped

 November
No

 Oscar
Man Overboard

 Papa
About to Sail

 Quebec
Request Pratique

 Romeo
The Way is Off My Ship

 Sierra
Engines Going Astern

 **T**ango
Keep Clear of Me

 Uniform
Standing Into Danger

 Victor
Require Assistance

 Whiskey
Require Medical Assistance

 Xray
Stop Your Intention

 Yankee
Am Dragging Anchor

 Zulu
Require a Tug

 1st Repeat

 2nd Repeat

 3rd Repeat

1

2

3

4

5

6

7

8

9

0

QUICK REFERENCE GUIDE

SECTORS OF NAVIGATION

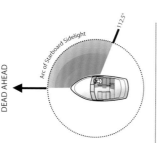

STARBOARD

112.5°

135°

PORT

STERN

OPERATING RULES:

PORT: If a power-driven boat approaches your boat from the port sector, you are the stand-on craft. Maintain your course and speed with caution.

STARBOARD: If a boat approaches your boat from the starboard sector, you are the give-way craft and must keep out of its way.

STERN: If another boat approaches you from the stern (from behind), you are the stand-on craft. Maintain your course and speed with caution.

THE DANGER ZONE (GIVE WAY ZONE)

Arc of Starboard Sidelight

112.5°

DEAD AHEAD

Your starboard sector (green sidelight) is the 'Danger Zone'. When another boat sees your green light, they will have the right-of-way. You must take early and substantial action to avoid a collision.

MARINE RADIO DISTRESS SIGNALS

DISTRESS CALL: USE 2182 KHZ OR CHANNEL 16, 156.8 MHZ (VHF)

- Repeat 'Mayday' three times to signal immediate danger (life threatening)
- Repeat 'Pan Pan' three times to indicate your need for help (non-life threatening)
- Provide information about your boat and the nature of the emergency

IF YOU ARE VESSEL A:

OVERTAKING

You have the right-of-way.

STARBOARD APPROACH

You do NOT have the right of way.

PORT APPROACH

You have the right-of-way.

APPROACHING NON-MOTORIZED BOATS:

Motorized boats NEVER have the right-of-way.

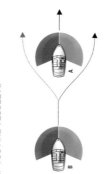

HEAD-ON APPROACH

Neither boat has the right-of-way (both boats must turn to their right to avoid a collision).

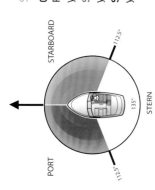

REMEMBER: Opposites attract when heading upstream! Your boat's green sidelight matches up with red buoys that your boat approaches, and your red starboard sidelight matches up with green buoys that your boat approaches. **RED/GREEN, GREEN/RED WHEN HEADING UP STREAM!**

QUICK REFERENCE GUIDE

BOATsmart!

THE LATERAL SYSTEM

STARBOARD (RED BUOYS)
Keep on the right side of your boat when heading upstream.

PORT (GREEN BUOYS)
Keep on the left side of your boat when heading upstream.

MEMORY TIP:
'RED RIGHT RETURNING'
KEEP THE RED BUOY ON THE RIGHT SIDE WHEN RETURNING UPSTREAM

STARBOARD-JUNCTION BIFURCATION BUOY:
The preferred channel is to the left.

BIFURCATION (RED & GREEN BUOYS)
Pass on either side when heading upstream but the main or preferred channel is indicated by the colour of the topmost band.

PORT-JUNCTION BIFURCATION BUOY:
The preferred channel is to the right.

FAIRWAY BUOY
Marks the entrance to a channel, the center of a shipping channel or a safe approach to land. Keep it on the left side of your boat whether proceeding upstream or downstream.

ISOLATED DANGER BUOY
Used to mark an isolated hazard or obstruction such as a rock, shoal or sunken island. Steer well clear of marked danger.

CARDINAL BUOYS
Identifies safe water in the direction indicated by the buoy-on either the north, south, east or west side.

 NORTH

 SOUTH EAST WEST

DAY BEACONS

PORT-HAND DAY BEACON
Keep on the left side of your boat when heading upstream.

STARBOARD-HAND DAY BEACON:
Keep on the right side of your boat when heading upstream.

PORT JUNCTION DAY BEACON
Marks the junction of two channels and may be passed on either side. If the preferred channel is desired, then keep it on the left side of the boat when heading upstream.

STARBOARD JUNCTION DAY BEACON
Marks the junction of two channels and may be passed on either side. If the preferred channel is desired, then keep it on the right side of the boat when heading upstream.